FROM INDIA
TO
AMERICA

A Brief History of Immigration;
Problems of Discrimination;
Admission and Assimilation

EDITED BY
S. CHANDRASEKHAR

FROM INDIA
TO
AMERICA

A Brief History of Immigration;
Problems of Discrimination;
Admission and Assimilation

EDITED BY
S. CHANDRASEKHAR

A POPULATION REVIEW BOOK
LA JOLLA, CALIFORNIA

Published in the United States of America 1982
by Population Review Publications
8976 Cliffridge Avenue
La Jolla, California 92037

Library of Congress Cataloging in Publication Data

Chandrasekhar, Sripati (editor)
FROM INDIA TO AMERICA

1. history of immigration from India to the U.S.

2. immigrant communities from India in the U.S. — problems

3. statistics of immigration 4. assimilation and Americanization
   bibliography

Library of Congress Catalog Card Number 82-60824

International Standard Book Number 0-9609080-0-5

Printed in the United States of America

PREFACE

The idea for this volume of essays on the history of immigration from India to the United States, and the Indian immigrant communities and their problems in this country, arose out of a graduate course on "International Migration" that I was invited to offer at the Population Research Laboratory, Department of Sociology, University of Southern California, in 1981.

The students, besides native Americans, were from more than fifteen foreign countries, including India; some were expecting to return to their own countries and some were immigrants to the U.S. They brought a variety of interesting national backgrounds to the class discussions.

The course revealed that while there was a plethora of books on various European national immigrant groups in the U.S., the Asians had not been studied adequately, and the Indians not at all.

While studies on Chinese and Japanese immigration were not entirely wanting, there was not a single book on the history and growth of the slender Indian immigration to the U.S. and the small pockets of Indian immigrant communities. Hence this introductory volume.

I am indebted to all the contributors who readily responded to my request to write papers specially for this volume. In fact, almost all the contributors are engaged in researching books on various aspects of Indian immigration to and immigrant life in the U.S. The readers of this survey may well look forward to the publication of these books.

I am indebted to Professors William Petersen and David M. Heer for their valuable suggestions.

S. Chandrasekhar

Department of Social Ecology
University of California, Irvine

To the memory of the pioneering Asian Indian immigrants to the United States of America, particulary the Sikhs from the Punjab, who braved a hostile environment at the turn of the century.

FROM INDIA TO AMERICA

Also by S. Chandrasekhar

"A Dirty, Filthy Book": the writings of Charles Knowlton and Annie Besant on birth control and an account of the Bradlaugh-Besant trial. (Berkeley and London: University of California Press, 1981).

The Nagarathars of South India An Essay and a Bibliography (Madras: Macmillan, 1980).

Population and Law in India (Madras: Macmillan, 1978) Revised enlarged edition.

Ananda K. Coomaraswamy (1877-1947): A Critical Appreciation (Madras: Blackie and Son, 1977).

Abortion in a Crowded World: The Problem of Abortion with Special Reference to India Foreword by Professor Garrett Hardin (London: Allen and Unwin; Seattle: University of Washington Press, 1974).

Infant Mortality, Population Growth and Family Planning in India (London; Allen and Unwin, 1972; Chapel Hill: The University of North Carolina Press, 1975) Second edition.

India's Population: Facts, Problems and Policies (Meerut, India: Meenakshi Prakashan, 1970) Second edition.

Asia's Population Problems (London: Allen and Unwin, 1967; Westport; Greenwood Press, 1977) Second edition.

Problems in Economic Development (edited), (Boston: D.C. Heath, 1967).

American Aid and India's Economic Development (London: Pall Mall Press: New York: Praeger, 1966) Third printing.

Red China: An Asian View (New York: Praeger, 1964) Fifth printing.

Communist China Today (London: Asia Publishing House, 1964) Third enlarged edition.

A Decade of Mao's China (edited), (Bombay: The Perennial Press, 1962).

China's Population: Census and Vital Statistics (Hong Kong: Hong Kong University Press, 1962; New York: Oxford University Press, 1962) Second revised edition.

A Report on South Indian Reading Habits (Madras: Southern Languages Book Trust and Ford Foundation, 1960).

Infant Mortality in India, 1901-1955 Foreword by Philip M. Hauser (London: Allen and Unwin; New York, Humanities Press, 1959.

Report on a Survey of Attitudes of Married Couples toward Family Planning in the City of Madras (Madras: Government of Madras Press, 1958).

Indians in South Africa: A Survey (Madras: Indian Institute for Population Studies, 1957).

Population and Planned Parenthood in India Forewords by Jawaharlal Nehru and Julian Huxley (London: Allen and Unwin, 1956; New York: Macmillan, 1956) Second revised edition.

Hungry People and Empty Lands Introduction by William Vogt (London: Allen and Unwin; New York: Macmillan, 1955) Third edition.

India's Population: Fact and Policy Foreword by Warren S. Thompson (New York: John Day, 1946) Second edition 1950.

Census and Statistics in India (Chidambaram: Annamalai University Press 1948).

Indian Emigration to America (Bombay: Oxford University Press, 1947).

India and the War (New York: News India, 1942).

of Related Interest

Ashish Bose et al (eds.): Studies in Demography: Essays in honour of S. Chandrasekhar (London: Allen and Unwin, 1971; Chapel Hill: The University of North Carolina Press, 1974) Fourth printing.

CONTENTS

page

PREFACE

LIST OF TABLES

1. A History of United States Legislation with Respect
   to Immigration from India   11
   S. CHANDRASEKHAR

2. The Asian Indian Immigrants in the United States, 1900-1965   29
   GARY R. HESS

3. Administrative Restriction of Asian Indian Immigration
   into the United States, 1907-1917   35
   HAROLD S. JACOBY

4. Revolution in India: Made in America   41
   EMILY C. BROWN

5. The Gadar Syndrome: Ethnic Anger and Nationalist Pride   48
   MARK JUERGENSMEYER

6. Immigration Law and the Revitalization Process: The Case of the
   California Sikhs   59
   BRUCE LA BRACK

7. Marriage and Family Life Among Early Asian Indian Immigrants   67
   KAREN LEONARD

8. Asian Indian Americans — Search for an Economic Profile   76
   MANORANJAN DUTTA

9. Some Statistics on Asian Indian Americans in the United States   86
   S. CHANDRASEKHAR

10. A Bibliography of Asian Indians in the United States:
    History of Immigration and Immigrant Communities in the
    United States   93
    S. CHANDRASEKHAR

ABOUT THE CONTRIBUTORS   107

INDEX   109

LIST OF TABLES

page

1. Annual Number and Percentage of East Indians Debarred from Entering U.S. at Ports of Entry, 1906-1915   37

2. Asian Indian Immigration into the U.S., 1899-1913   41

3. Chart on Punjab Politics   50

4. Effect of the 1965 Act on Asian Indian Population Growth in the U.S. to 1975   62

5. Occupational Status of Arriving Asian Indian Immigrants   62

6. Reported Residence of Asian Indians on Permanent Status   63

7. Distribution of Asian Indian Immigrants by Reported Residence in California   63

8. Asian Indian Population Estimates for Yuba City   64

9. Sikh Vital Statistics, 1905-1939   68

10. Map — California Counties, 1974   69

11. Ethnicity and County of Wives   71

12. Regional Distribution of Asian Indians   78

13. Groups of States with Varying Sizes of Asian Indian Population   78

14. Asian/Pacific Americans and Asian Indians   79

15. Immigrant Arrivals in the U.S. of Persons Reporting India as a Nation of Last Permanent Residence, 1820-1977   87

16. Immigrant Arrivals in the U.S. Born in India, 1870-1970   88

17. Immigration to the U.S. from India, 1820-1978   88

18. Persons of Indian Birth Admitted to the U.S., 1971-1978   89

TABLES (Continued)

page

19.   Immigrants from India Admitted to the U.S. in 1978, by Classes   89

20.   Immigrants from India Admitted to the U.S., Under Numerical Limitation
     by Preference, 1978   90

21.   Immigrants of Indian Birth Admitted to the U.S. in 1978
     by Occupation Groups   90

22.   Immigrants of Indian Birth Admitted to the U.S. in 1978
     by Sex and Age   91

23.   Non-Immigrants of Indian Birth Admitted to the U.S. in 1978 by Classes   91

24.   Aliens of Indian Birth Who Reported Under the Alien Address
     Program, 1976-1979   92

25.   Asian Indians in the U.S., 1980   92

"One law shall be to him that is home-born and unto the stranger that soujourneth among you."

Exodus 12:49

"The stranger that soujourneth with you shall be unto you as the home-born among you."

Leviticus 15:34

"The bosom of America is open to receive not only the Opulent and Respectable Stranger but the oppressed and persecuted of all Nations and Religions; Whom we shall welcome to a participation of all our rights and privileges, if by decency and propriety of conduct they appear to merit the enjoyment."

George Washington, December 2, 1783, New York, John C. Fitzpatrick (ed.) *The Writings of George Washington; from the Original Manuscript Sources; 1745-1779* (Washington, D.C.: U.S. Government Printing Office, 1938) Vol. 28, p. 254.

A History of United States Legislation
With Respect to Immigration from India[1]

by

S. Chandrasekhar*

"A measure of greatness for any nation is its ability to recognize past errors in judgment and its willingness to reform its public policy." — Senator Edward M. Kennedy (1966)

This essay attempts to trace briefly the history of the immigration of the nationals of India[2], or what was the sub-continent of India before partition, to the United States of America, through all its unpredictable vicissitudes of welcome and refusal, admission and denial, prejudice and tolerance, negative and positive legislative Acts and court decisions.

Though the Asian story begins about a century ago, the Indian part of it commences from the turn of the century. In a word, the American legislative history concerning immigration from the overall Asian point of view can be summed up simply as a classic century-old instance of professed American ideals of democracy and freedom on the one hand, and the practical realities of rank prejudice and flagrant discrimination on the other. However, the last major U.S. Immigration Act, of 1965, put an end to this sad story and the period of discriminatory selective immigration is over. People are now permitted to come from every part of the world, with an established limitation of 20,000 as the number of the quota to be filled by citizens of any one nation, irrespective of color, creed, ethnic or national origin.

In recounting this brief history of Indian immigration, students of Asian and international affairs have seldom attempted to correlate the relation between American discriminatory immigration laws vis-a-vis major Asian countries, and Asia's hostile reactions to American interests in Asia. This needs to be done for it would offer insights valuable to the formation of wise American foreign policy.

One hopes that the long sullen relationship between Asia and the United States has come to an end, and that America has learned to eschew forever any posture of white supremacy or racial superiority over any other people in the world today. The United States, like any other nation large or small, free or Communist, has her legitimate interests and every right to pursue them through every available channel of international law, without injecting indirectly or even remotely any claim of superiority based on "race", color or religion.

The Period of Free Immigration: 1776 - 1882

When the population of the United States was growing relatively rapidly largely because of immigration during the first century of its foundation as an independent nation, neither the government nor the people who gave thought to these matters considered seriously the subject of immigration into the U.S. as a controllable phenomenon, if it needed any control at all.

In fact, from the Declaration of Independence in 1776 to 1882, the U.S. Government had no policy of control or restriction over immigration into or emigration from the United States of America. That is, since the adoption of the Constitution in 1789 the U.S. did not have any immigration laws and it was assumed that open doors and open borders were the natural order of things.

It is true that some states had certain ad hoc immigration restrictions to ease local "problems." For instance, a few states along the Atlantic seaboard, New York, New Jersey and Pennsylvania, had their own "immigration laws", and California and other states on the West Coast petitioned Congress to institute measures to control immigration. But there were no federal immigration laws other than those passed to assist immigration and to safeguard the welfare of the immigrants, particularly during their trans-Atlantic voyages.[3]

The Supreme Court ruled that the states had no authority to levy head taxes on aliens entering various states as immigrants. In 1875 the Court pointed out the division of power between the states and the federal government and declared that the immigration regulations that certain states passed "infringed on Congress's exclusive power over foreign commerce."[4]

The Possible First Arrival From India in the United States

We do not know for certain who the first arrival was — immigrant or temporary visitor — from India to the United States. Was it a single person, a family or a group? To what cultural-linguistic group did this enterprising first arrival from India belong? We have no precise answers to these questions. But, as far as we know, the first arrival may have come from Madras in South India.

This earliest record of the presence of an Asian Indian in North America is to be found in a colonial diary. In 1790 an Indian from Madras visited Salem, Massachusetts (could he possibly have come from Salem, South India?) He is believed to have accompanied a British sea captain who was plying a trading vessel between New England ports and such coastal towns as Bombay, Madras and Calcutta. One Rev. William Bentley, a Salem, Massachusetts clergyman, wrote in his diary for December 29, 1790, "Had the pleasure of seeing for the first time a native of the Indies from Madras. He is of dark complexion, long straight black hair, soft countenance, tall and well proportioned. He is said to be darker than Indians in general of his own caste, being much darker than any native Indians of America. I had no opportunity to judge of his ability but his countenance was not expressive. He came to Salem with Capt. J. Gibaut, and has been in Europe."[5]

Unfortunately, we are not told whether the Indian from Madras remained in Salem or just passed through. However, it may be surmised that this was the beginning of the subsequent arrival of a small group of Asian Indians in Salem. Sixty-one years later we have a report that in Salem in 1851 half a dozen Asian Indians participated in the July 4th parade of the East India Marine Society.[6]

A Parsi Episode

Of the various ethnic elements that go to make up the business community in India, the Parsis of Bombay, though a small religious minority, constitute an elite and relatively wealthy group. They are the descendants of the Persians (present day Iranians) of the Zoroastrian faith who fled to India in the seventh century rather than be forcibly converted to Islam.

The total population of the whole Parsi community in 1870, the decade when the first official but incomplete census of the country was taken, must have been considerably less than 100,000. The total population of India (for the undivided area including Pakistan and Bangladesh) according to the first Indian 1871-72 census was 190 million, so the Parsis constituted a tiny minority of the nation's population.

Because of their role as middlemen for the Portugese and British traders during the heyday of the British East India Company, they became by the end of the eighteenth century an affluent business community in India. They were not only successful businessmen who helped in laying the foundations of India's industrialization (they gave the house of Tatas to the Indian business world), but they took an active part in the nationalist struggle for the country's political freedom. From the Parsi community came Dadabhai Naoroji (1825-1917), the "Grand Old Man" of Indian nationalism, as well as brilliant lawyer nationalist, Ferozshah Mehta (1845-1915), and several lesser luminaries.

Their close association with British and other European businessmen resulted in their being the first Indian community to become westernized. Soon they were trying to build business relations with the latest foreign arrivals in Bombay — the Americans.

While the United States Government had expressed its desire to open consular offices in India after George Washington became the President of the infant republic, British intransigence prevented the opening of U.S. consulates at any Indian port cities for more than half a century. It was not until 1838 that consular relations were established and it took about two decades more before the local governments in India gave legal recognition to the American consular representative in Bombay. The trade between India and the United States was just beginning and the only American commodity demanded in India then was natural ice (dug out of Boston lakes) for the needs of European residents in tropical India! The exports from India to the United States were piece goods, and hides and skins. The number of Americans including those in the U.S. consular establishments at the Indian port cities was small. In fact the consular offices were manned for many years by some prominent American merchant in India and not by any foreign service staff recruited in the United States.

The Parsis were the first Indian community in Bombay to establish close relations with the American consul there. A leading Parsi businessman, Dossabhoy Merwanji, who had visited the United States more than once and was familiar with American business and trade conditions as well as consular rules and regulations, was among the first to befriend Edward Ely, the first American consular official to be recognized by the British authorities in Bombay. Ely was so impressed with Merwanji's knowledge of the United States and his pro-American attitude that when he had to return home in 1852 due to illness and financial distress, he appointed Merwanji, "to act in my name as Vice-Consul of the United States at Bombay, I'm holding myself responsible for all his acts and fidelity." Consuls at that time received no salaries and the consular fees collected from the American ships visiting the port were woefully inadequate to meet their expenses. Ely wrote to then Secretary of State Daniel Webster, " In the absence of Americans at this place I have preferred him (Merwanji) to any English merchant resident."[7]

In 1888 another Parsi, Hormusji E. Bode, was appointed American Vice-Consul in Bombay; and when the consul suddenly died in August 1889 it was Bode who continued to hold responsibilities until the arrival of the new American consul, Harry Ballantine in October 1898.

The available records of the period suggest that the Bombay Parsis were among the largest single group of Indian businessmen carrying on export-import trade with the U.S. And as a consequence they took a keen interest in the work of the U.S. consulate, to the extent of writing to the Secretary of State on one occasion pleading for the retention of a particular consul when the local Americans were against him.

While the majority of the Parsis lived and worked in Bombay City, a few hundred families were settled in such upcountry towns as Baroda and Surat. (Incidentally, it was in Surat that the British merchants of the East India Company originally settled and erected their first factory.) The leaders of the Baroda branch of the community which had been settled in India for more than ten centuries, were exploring newer and greener pastures for the community's growth and prosperity. Incredible as it may sound, the Parsis of Baroda in the 1870's were actually seriously considering emigrating to the United States, not individually or in small numbers comprising a few families but en masse as a total community.

Indian emigration to certain regions of the British Empire both in Asia and Africa in search of better jobs and higher standards of living was not unknown then. The example that might have inspired the Parsis of Baroda was perhaps the Gujaratis, among whom they were settled in Western India and whose language they spoke as their mother tongue. The Gujaratis — both Hindus and Muslims — had begun emigrating from the Bombay region to such British colonies in central Africa as Kenya, Uganda, Malawi, Rhodesia and Zambia in quest of new homes and better business opportunities. The colonial Africans had not yet come into their own and the Gujarati Indians became not only successful independent businessmen but entered into various British colonial administrations in the middle level official posts as junior civil servants, teachers, office superintendents, clerks, etc.

But the Parsis of Baroda, and the Bombay area as a whole, felt they were more westernized and wished to explore wider horizons for their business enterprise and entrepreneurial ability. But they had no first hand information about conditions in the contemporary United States — climate and food, cost of land and housing and the exact range of business and trading opportunities, and jobs in general — beyond that the

14

United States was a growing nation of immigrants, a land of exceptional opportunities, and *theoretically* anyone from anywhere could come to the United States and make good by hard work and perseverance.

In the United States it was still the period of free immigration (1776-1882) and the Chinese Exclusion Act had not yet been passed.

The immigrants from the south and central European countries, who were flocking to the United States in the thousands during that period, had countless friends and relatives already in the United States writing to them generally favorable letters with all kinds of information on which they could base their judgements. The shipping lines were not recruiting people from India, as they were from China; nor was there in the United States an already established immigrant Indian community. During the period in question less than a dozen Indians were going to the United States for permanent residence, and less than 200 Indians had emigrated to the United States during the half century preceding 1870. America was far away, halfway round the world, and the ships from Bombay, Madras or Calcutta took three months to reach New York or San Francisco. So the Parsis were in need of first hand, and up-to-date information about conditions in the United States. It was these circumstances that led to the dispatch of the following letter by three leaders of the small Parsi community in Baroda addressed to the U.S. Consul Benjamin F. Farnham in Bombay in 1876, a century after the United States was founded as an independent republic.[8]

Cotton Ginning Factory
Baroda
30 August 1876

To
The American Consul
Bombay

Dear Sir,

Many enterprising and intelligent Parsees are desirous of emigrating to the New World and of establishing themselves as colonists on the same plan and system as Europeans [sic] settlers have been doing. It is a thought uppermost in the minds of some of our Community to form themselves into a body and by so doing to invest a certain Amount of their own Capital in purchasing Cultivable lands of Considerable Area. The principal object of such an investment is to found a separate Colony of Parsees only in a land which has been from times immemorial the fostering nurse of many an enterprising and needy adventurer and well-to-do Capitalist where they Can without the slightest impediment preserve and follow the religion of their forefathers. But they are not sufficiently informed as to the climate, resources and husbandry of the very vast country of the United States and the little knowledge they are in a position of obtaining from several books and pamphlets is so uncertain and so unreliable that it fails to make a vivid impression on their minds and attract them directly to the subject.

We the undersigned therefore deem you the Constituted representative of the Independent States as the chief and very reliable source of all authentic information in the matter. You are perhaps already aware that the Parsees of Western India do not fall even a whit behind their immediate neighbors the Englishmen and their distant fellow-men the Europeans wherever the Spirit of noble enterprise and great undertakings is concerned. A settlement in America at the earliest opportunity has become the subject of our grave considerations, but our minds are not sufficiently enlightened in it as they ought to be. Being placed in a position of the full particulars which we request you to supply us with we intend to lay before our Community in public lectures and Journals all the advantages derivable from their monetary concerns, their social Connections and their taking part in a system of politics by making the foreign but cherished country as their new home and permanent domicile. But for a successful achievement of our plan and rendering our information and arguments unimpeachable we indispensably need your able support and Cooperation. We fully comprehend the usefulness of all such informations [sic] supplied by you, and we can not but appreciate their full values which is really uncomparable [sic] to that of all Knowledge we can by dint of exertion and Close applications gather from writers and authorities. We shall therefore feel ourselves highly obliged by your favouring us at your earliest convenience with all particulars or references for such particulars as are of paramount importance to us in the Carrying out of our somewhat arduous scheme and with the successful accomplishment your name shall be associated with grateful rememberance by all those who will in future profit thereby.

We remain etc.

Signed   Roostumjee Mehrwanji N
          (Narelwala)
  ''   Sorabjee Muncherjee
          Master
  ''   Eduljee Jamsetjee
          Nehory

"The letter is significant in many ways," comments Professor Tripathi. "First, it reveals that the Parsi plan for emigration was prompted by the same economic motive which was the guiding force behind the European migration to the United States in the 19th century. Secondly, this was perhaps the only attempt ever made by Indians to emigrate in a group with a view of forming a settlement of their own in the New World.[9] Thirdly, the letter indicates that behind the apparent goodwill and admiration that the Parsis had for the British in India was a hidden discontent and latent resentment born out of a sense of discrimination they thought they were subjected to under an alien rule. And lastly, the Parsi communication gives some idea of the Indian image of the United States in the latter half of the 19th century.[10]

The Burlingame Treaty of 1868

The first American laws concerning the movement of Asians — the Chinese, in this case — into the United States was the Burlingame Treaty of 1868, named after Anson Burlingame, the first American Minister to China, who negotiated the treaty.

To begin with, this Treaty was devoid of honest intentions on America's part because it was negotiated solely to enable Americans to reside in and trade with China. Since China then was a sovereign nation, no matter how nominal the sovereignty, the American Government had to introduce the necessary clause of reciprocity, a token one, no doubt, and hence the promise to let Chinese come to America, if Americans were to be let into China. The American Government of the day with typical, if superior short sight, hoped the reciprocity would be an empty gesture and could not (or did not) conceive of the possibility of Chinese emigration to the United States.

The preamble of the Treaty reads: "The United States of America and the Emperor of China cordially recognize the inherent and inalienable right of man to change his home and allegiance and also the mutual advantage of the free migration and emigration of their citizens and subjects respectively, from one country to the other, for the purpose of curiosity, of trade, or as permanent residents.[11]

This treaty became the target of the residents in California, particularly the unskilled Irish immigrants, who as laborers competed with the Chinese and bitterly resented their presence, until the Chinese Exclusion Act was passed; and for a few decades thereafter, until the passage of the Immigration Act of 1924 which prohibited the immigration of aliens (the Chinese and others) ineligible for naturalization.

The Chinese Exclusion Act of 1882

The history of U.S. Legislation with respect to Asian Indians must be understood in the context of legislation concerning the immigration of other Asians. Asian immigration to the United States, when it began, was largely limited to the Pacific Coast states. While a great many of the immigrants from the Pacific Asian countries headed for California, a small number trickled into Oregon and Washington states. In volume the Asian arrivals constituted a small and slender stream of a few thousand compared to the immense uncontrolled flood of millions of European immigrants.

Three significant facts must be remembered in connection with Asian immigration to the United States. First, California has been part of the United States of America for only 132 years, while the Asian countries facing or adjoining the Pacific had civilizations four to five thousand years old. Second, California was a Mexican province until 1846 and the center of political and administrative power was in the far south in Mexico City. The Mexican War of 1846-1848 led to political annexation of California to the United States. And last, the discovery of gold in 1848 had brought many of the dregs of rootless white humanity from the east coast of the United States, and from Europe and Australia to California in search of a quick fortune.

While the pauper polyglot adventurers were obsessed with their digging in lawless communities, there were few people available for the hard labor of building new communities. It was this scarcity of labor, menial and otherwise, in California at this time, as well as the perennially over-populated Chinese southern province of Kwantung, that paved the way for the beginnings of Chinese immigration into the United States.

While agents of both the Pacific Coast shipping and the Pacific railroad construction companies induced Chinese laborers to come, mostly from Canton in Kwantung province and Honkong, they were not always welcomed when they did arrive. Though the Chinese recruits worked hard and on low wages in relation to both the native and immigrant white workers, their presence, the Chinese way of life and their frugal habits, evoked hostility and even violent opposition in the 1860's and 1870's. Soon several local ordinances and state laws discriminating against the Chinese were passed.[12]

China, a nominally independent and sovereign nation, but militarily and otherwise weak, protested this discriminatory attitude towards her nationals, particularly since she had treaty rights with the United States. But the opposition to the Chinese laborers on the West Coast was considerable. In fact, in 1879 the California electorate voted 154,638 to 833 to end further Chinese immigration into California. The Congress passed two bills between 1879 and 1882 banning Chinese immigration but they were vetoed as they violated the existing American treaty with China. Therefore the United States was compelled to negotiate a new treaty in 1880 by which China agreed to the exclusion of her nationals from American shores with the exception of the conventional category of students, businessmen and visitors. Thus the Chinese Exclusion Act was passed in May 1882 which debarred Chinese immigrant labor for ten years and prevented Chinese aliens from obtaining United States citizenship.

The Act was renewed in 1892 for a similar period and made quasi-permanent in 1904. Thirty-nine years later, during the Second World War, Japanese war propaganda and broadcasts were making pointed fun of the United States championing China when she did not even admit Chinese to her shores, much less permit them to become naturalized citizens. The Congress repealed the Chinese Exclusion Act in 1943 and made the Chinese eligible for both immigration and naturalization. But the Chinese had to wait for the Japanese attack on Pearl Harbor to become immigrants to the United States.

Thus the Chinese Exclusion Act of 1882, which was the first piece of restrictive immigration legislation in American history (and which banned not only Chinese immigration but also eliminated the possibility of anyone of Chinese ancestry becoming a citizen of the U.S.) set the stage for discrimination against all Asians for some eighty-three years. In fact, successive administrators confided to authorities in India that they could not very well permit Indians to become regular immigrants to the U.S. without at the same time lifting the barriers against the Chinese.

The Alien Contract Labor Law of 1885

During the 1880's various American labor organizations had been vocal in complaining that several American employers, particularly on the West Coast, were importing workers who were willing to work at relatively low wages compared to native American, or earlier immigrant workers. This agitation was directed primarily against employers importing Asian workers by alleged misrepresentation of job opportunities in the United States. The labor organizations did not agitate for minimum wages for all workers but for the ban on the arrival of what was called "cheap labor". No one apparently took into consideration that every worker would like to receive the highest possible wages.

However, in response to these complaints, the United States Congress passed in 1885 and in 1887 the Alien Contract Labor Law (Act of February 26, 1885 and Act of February 23, 1887.) These Acts made the importation of aliens under contract for the performance of labor or other specified services illegal. Those who came to work temporarily as artists, lecturers, servants and skilled workers in an industry not yet established in the United States were exempted.

An amendment to these laws in 1888 (Act of October 19, 1888) provided for the expulsion of any alien, for the first time since the 1798 Act,[13] within one year of his or her entry in violation of the contract labor laws. The Supreme Court in 1893 (Lees v. United States) upheld the constitutionality of this Act as amended.

The Immigration Act of 1907 (The Gentlemen's Agreement with Japan) (1907-1920)

The story of Japanese immigration into the United States is not entirely dissimilar to that of the Chinese. Whether or not the rulers of Japan were aware of the existence of the Americas, they were content within their islands. Japan did not come seeking entry into America. It was the American Commodore Matthew C. Perry who arrived at Gore-Hama in 1853 seeking trade relations with Japan.

The beginning of trade relations paved the way for the arrival of Japanese laborers as immigrants. It was in 1885 when the Japanese emperor removed a long-standing ban on the emigration of his subjects that the first group of 148 Japanese immigrants — contract agricultural laborers — arrived in Hawaii. They came without their families but when they found jobs and got settled, their wives and children joined them. Later, some returned to Japan while others moved to California, for the U.S. in 1898 had annexed Hawaii and the Hawaiian residents were free to move to the continental United States. Between 1885 and 1900 less than 12,000 had arrived, but about 90,000 came during the next decade. Soon the Japanese had to face the same prejudice and discrimination that

the Chinese had encountered earlier, and here with even less justification. When the rabble-rousing California politicians became successful in excluding the Chinese, they saw no reason why the Japanese should not be kept out as well. An attempt to cover up the corruption and graft of certain California politicians at that time was one of the reasons that led to the ban on the arrival of immigrants from Japan. Oscar Handlin, the distinguished American historian, explains and as this bit of history is not widely known, it is worth quoting:

> There had been some calls for the exclusion of the Nipponese in 1901. But the question became serious in 1905 when Mayor Eugene F. Schmitz and Abraham Ruef, the bosses of the dominant San Francisco political machines, ordered ninety-three Japanese children into segregated schools. They did so in order to divert attention from the findings of a grand jury then investigating the misdeeds of the municipal government. But the calls to prejudice found a responsive audience, and anti-Japanese sentiments spread like wildfire.
>
> The commotion embarrassed the national administration, which had been working for a diplomatic understanding with Japan in the interest of collaboration in the Far East. President Theodore Roosevelt, eager to soothe ruffled feelings in Tokyo without antagonising California voters, sponsored an informal "Gentlemen's Agreement" in 1907-1908, by which the Japanese government undertook to prevent laborers from leaving for the United States in return for the assurance that American law would not stigmatize the Mikado's subjects as inferiors. Such voluntary restraint, did not, however, appease the prejudiced on the Pacific Coast. Local land and school statutes discriminated against the Japanese, and, periodically, fulmination in the press and from the podium warned that the "little yellow men" were bringing in picture brides with the intention of multiplying to take over the country.[14]

The Gentlemen's Agreement permitted the entry of parents, wives or children of Japanese residents of the U.S. But there were many single males legally resident in California who could not get Japanese brides from the small Japanese community in California. And hence the Japanese male in the United States would arrange for a marriage with a woman in Japan by proxy, knowing her only by a photograph supplied by a marriage broker. These "picture brides" could then legally enter the country to marry. To an Asian who is living alone and who desires to marry within his ethnic group, and who is prevented from going back to his native country to choose a bride, this system did not appear absurd. (It is a time-honored custom in Asia for the family rather than the individual to decide upon a suitable marriage partner.) But to the anti-Japanese American this marriage system was seen as a subversive method to increase the Japanese population in California.[15]

In 1920 the system of obtaining picture brides was made illegal. Two years later Japanese aliens in the United States were declared ineligible for citizenship. And in 1924 in the Immigration Act based on the quota system, Japan was given no quota and as such Japanese immigration was virtually stopped from that year.

The Immigration Act of 1917

Apart from the Gentlemen's Agreement with Japan, the 1907 Immigration Act created a Joint Commission on Immigration consisting of three members each from both the Senate and the House of Representatives and three additional outside members to investigate and report on the immigration system of the United States. The resulting report of the Commission was published in forty-two volumes in 1911. The pages reveal the profound ignorance of the authors, and much racial nonsense based on nothing more than simple prejudice was passed off as "scientific knowledge". On the race question the report's views were more superstitious than scientific judged even by the limited knowledge of the day.

The Immigration Act of 1917 was based on the dubious knowledge of this voluminous report, and the U.S. immigration law basically was unaltered until the Act of 1952.

This Act included some previous exclusion provisions, and added to the list of inadmissible aliens illiterates, constitutional psychopaths, chronic alcoholics, stowaways, vagrants and individuals with a previous attack of insanity.

Two provisions of the Act were controversial. One clause imposed further restrictions on the immigration of aliens by the creation of a "Pacific Barred Zone", the natives of which were declared inadmissible to the United States. It was not clear who the learned pandits were who devised this barred zone, nor was anyone clear on what criteria it was based. It included most of China (the Chinese were already excluded, as were the Japanese), India, Burma, Siam, the Malay States, the Asian part of Russia, most of Arabia, Afghanistan, the Polynesian islands and the East Indian islands (present Indonesia).

Critics who examined the Act in some detail at the time offered two plausible explanations for the barred zone. One was that the United States Government, having discriminated against two important countries, China and Japan, did not wish these countries to feel that they had been singled out for discrimination, and so they added India and the rest for the sake of fairness!

A second explanation was that the nefarious hand of British imperialism was visible. Some American critics have felt that the Congress and the immigration authorities often sought the advice of the British about nationals of the British colonial empire. This lack of independence in American judgment and a need to hang onto British skirts on this subject, occasioned by a determination not to hurt the sensitivities of her closest ally, which were very delicate wherever British colonials were concerned, has been pointed out by more than one critic.

The view of the British Government was simple enough: any national of their colonial empire in Asia, and particularly the educated and articulate Indians, if admitted to the U.S. would certainly carry on propaganda against British rule. This was a thorn in British flesh which they could well do without. But it was sad that the United States, which had fought British imperialism and won independence herself, could not sympathise with and support Indians and other colonials in their fight for their lost political freedom.

The second controversial clause of the 1917 Act pertained to the literacy test by which prospective immigrants over sixteen years of age who were unable to pass such a test were debarred. This clause, however, was not new, for a bill providing a literacy test was passed by Congress as early as 1897, vetoed by President Cleveland, and subsequent similar legislation was vetoed by Presidents Taft and Wilson. The 1917 Act containing the literacy requirement was passed over President Wilson's veto.

The Thind Case (1923)[16]

From about 1907 India's nationals had begun to enter the United States of America in quest of jobs and new opportunities. Many of them came from the province of British Columbia, Canada, where they had been working earlier, preferring the warmer California climate to the cold and rainy one of the Canadian West Coast.

Having entered legally, these newcomers applied for U.S. citizenship. Some obtained it and some did not. Thereupon a controversy arose over the question of the eligibility of Asian Indians for American citizenship.

The Asian Indians, like other people in older civilizations, profess many religions. The major religion in India, however, is Hinduism, and the minority religious groups belong to such faiths as Islam, Christianity, Sikhism and Buddhism, etc. The majority of the arrivals in the first few groups from India belonged to the Sikh faith, which may be described as a protestant combination of the good in the Hindu and Moslem faiths.

The first case of an unsuccessful application for U.S. citizenship, in California according to the available records, belongs to a Sikh immigrant, one Veer Singh. He applied for first papers at the County Clerk's office, Alameda, California in 1907. According to the records he would have become an American citizen, but Singh refused to remove his turban, in accordance with Sikh religious principles, while being sworn. His application was rejected, but the rejection was a matter of "manners" and was not related to the citizenship law.[17]

During the next fifteen years, between 1908 and 1923, some sixty-seven nationals of India who were legally admitted into the United States acquired citizenship through court procedures in no less than thirty-two courts in seventeen different states — from New York to Louisiana. One would have expected that so many court decisions conferring citizenship rights on Indian nationals would have acquired the status of Law and the issue would have been closed.

But apparently this was not to be the case. There was an initial opposition to the acquisition of citizenship rights by Indian residents in the United States even in 1907 from the U.S. Attorney General and the Federal Immigration and Naturalization Service, but this was dismissed by those who gave any thought to the subject as the unwilling response of U.S. agencies and officials to the unofficial pressure from the British embassy in Washington, D.C. And until 1923 the U.S. courts gave their judgements presumably on the merits of the various individual cases presented to them. It is also possible that during the same period some Indian applicants for the grant of citizenship were refused by the courts, though the record of the exact number, if any, of such rejections, is not readily available.

It must be pointed out, however, that there was some room for doubt about the eligibility of India's nationals for American citizenship. The Naturalization Law of 1790 limited the privilege to "free white persons" and an amendment passed in 1870 extended the right to "aliens of African nativity or persons of African descent." This was because of the importation of a large number of Negro slaves, and their descendants. This led eventually to the simple dichotomy, particularly in the south, of the American population as "white" and "colored", colored being Negroes, separate and unequal.

It must also be pointed out that Japanese and Chinese applicants for citizenship were denied the privilege by the lower courts in 1894 and 1895 on the basis of the 1790 Naturalization Law. The Indians were the only exceptions among Asians to receive a favorable verdict from the courts, on the assumption that they belonged to the same racial classification as "Europeans" and to "the Mediterranean branch of the Caucasian family", while the

Chinese and Japanese belonged to the Mongoloid group. This was the reasoning of many courts which granted Indians American citizenship.

For instance, Judge Charles E. Wolverton of the Oregon District Court, in 1920 points this out clearly when he decided in favor of Thind's application for citizenship. He said, "I am not disposed to discuss the question as one of first impression whether a high-class Hindu, coming from the Punjab is ethnologically a white person within the meaning of Section 2169 of the Revised Statutes . . . I am content to rest my decision of the question upon a line of cases of which (*In re: Mohan Singh* and *U.S. v. Balsara*) are illustrative. I am aware there are decisions to the contrary but am impressed that they are not in line with the greater weight of authority."[18]

An American student commenting on the Judge's remarks, observes, "That this point of view would prevail seemed especially likely by reason of the decision of the U.S. Supreme Court in 1922 in the case of *Ozawa v. U.S.* In this case, involving a Japanese, the Court officially equated the words 'white' and 'Caucasian' and while the decision definitely closed the door on the naturalization of Japanese, it seemed to assure the acceptance of 'Caucasians' from India as candidates for citizenship."[19]

A word about the Ozawa case as it precedes the Thind case and is akin to it. On November 13, 1922 Justice George Sutherland of the U.S. Supreme Court, delivering the Court's decision denying citizenship to Takao Ozawa, said, "The determination that the words, 'white person' are synonymous with the words, 'a person of the Caucasian race' simplified the problem, although it does not entirely dispose of it. Controversies have arisen and will no doubt arise again in respect of the proper classification of individuals in borderline cases."

The Immigration and Naturalization Service disagreed with the Oregon District Court and appealed Judge Wolverton's decision granting citizenship to Bhagat Singh Thind, a Sikh (not a Hindu) from the Punjab, and a First World War Veteran, to the United States Supreme Court.

On February 19, 1923, the same Justice Sutherland delivered the Court's opinion that Thind and consequently India's nationals were ineligible for U.S. citizenship. The learned Judge observed:

> "Caucasian" is a conventional word of much flexibility . . . and while it and the words "white persons" are treated as synonymous for the purpose [the Ozawa] case, they are not of identical meaning . . .
>
> In the endeavor to ascertain the meaning of the statute we must not fail to keep in mind that it does not employ the word "Caucasian" but the words "white persons", and these are words of common speech and not of scientific origin. The word "Caucasian" was not only not employed in the law but was probably wholly unfamiliar to the original framers of the statute in 1790 . . . in this country, during the last half century especially, the word (white person) by common usage has acquired a popular meaning not clearly defined to be sure, but sufficiently so to enable us to say that the popular, as distinguished from its scientific application, is of appreciably narrower scope . . . The words of the statute are to be interpreted in accordance with the understanding of the common man from whose vocabulary they were taken.[20]

Since the adverse verdict on both the Ozawa and the Thind cases depended on the precise meaning of the word "Caucasian" there was considerable anthropological, legal and semantic speculation at the time over Southerland's decision. Ray Chase and S. G. Pandit concluded that the test in the Ozawa case was race, not color, while in the Thind case the determination was color, not race.[21] The Justice's mental dexterity was confusing to say the least. The decision that the Indian nationals, in the opinion of the common man, were not Caucasians, whatever might be their race from the purely anthropological and biological points of view, was sustained solely on the racial prejudice of the "man in the street."[22]

In some cases the law was applied retroactively and American citizens who were formerly Indian nationals were required to surrender their American citizenship. But when the Immigration and Naturalization Service instituted proceedings against Sakharam G. Pandit, an Indian who was a U.S. citizen and a California attorney who had practiced law in both State and Federal courts, he opposed the proceedings with the plea of *res judicata*, that the original court in 1914 after hearing the government's protest to his application for citizenship, had granted him citizenship which was not then challenged. Pandit therefore contended that he was entitled to the 1914 decision which had been rendered by a court of competent jurisdiction. Both the district court and the circuit court of appeals subsequently agreed with Pandit, while the Supreme Court also agreed.[23]

In 1928 the citizenship of Shankar Laxman Gokhale of Schenectady, New York, a General Electric research engineer since 1912, was cancelled by District Appellate Court actions. Gokhale appealed to the United States Supreme Court. The Supreme Court granted a writ of Certiorari. The writ reversed the lower court actions and ordered the District Court to dismiss the bill of complaint entered earlier by the government. Gokhale was entitled to his citizenship and the lower courts had no power to revoke existing citizenship rights.[24]

The Immigration Act of 1924

In 1920-21 a demand for a drastic restriction of immigration arose to "guard against an influx of starving Europeans, whose arrival would flood an already depressed labor market." An official search for a formula was on — one that would eliminate the "new" immigration from southern and eastern Europe without affecting the "old". The Congress enacted a provisional emergency measure in May 1921, introducing quotas for the first time. The law restricted the number of immigrants of each nationality during the coming year to 3 percent of the number of foreign-born persons of that nationality resident in the United States during the last available census, that of 1910.

This temporary 1921 legislation, based very much on racism, was superseded by the Immigration Act of 1924 — the Johnson-Reed Act — or more popularly known as the Quota Act of 1924. The "scientific" basis for the quotas was provided by one Dr. Harry Laughlin,

a geneticist in the Eugenics Records Office, who was asked by the House Immigration Committee to prepare a report on the "new immigrants." He gave the committee his learned views in 1922 as follows: "We in this country have been so involved with the idea of democracy, or the equality of all men, that we have left out of consideration the matter of blood or natural born hereditary mental and moral differences. No man who breeds pedigreed plants and animals can affort to neglect this thing."[25]

Another expert, a psychologist, one Arthur Sweeney, reported to the House Committee on Immigration and Naturalization in 1923 as follows: "We cannot be seriously opposed to immigrants from Great Britain, Holland, Canada, Germany, Denmark and Scandinavia . . . We can, however, strenuously object to immigration from Italy . . . Russia . . . Poland . . . Greece . . . Turkey. The Slavic and Latin countries show a marked contrast in intelligence with the Western and Northern European group . . . they think with the spinal cord rather than the brain . . . We shall degenerate to the level of the Slav and Latin races . . . pauperism, crime, sex offenses, and dependency . . . guided by a mind scarcely superior to an ox."[26]

The committee, having satisfied itself that the immigrants from southern and eastern Europe were incapable of assimilation and were biologically inferior to the Nordic ethnic group of northern and western Europe, on the basis of the above expertise, devised the quotas in the Immigration Act of 1924.

Among the major provisions of this Act were:

1. The quota restrictions were no longer based on the percentage principle but on national origins.

2. The quota base was changed from the Census of 1910 to that of 1890 to further reduce immigration from southern and eastern Europe.

3. The quota admissible in any one year was reduced from 3 to 2 percent based on the 1890 census, thus lowering still further the proportion of south and east European entries.

4. The classes of aliens exempted from exclusion were reduced.

The quota laws of 1921 and 1924 also excluded Indians because of their belonging to the 1917 barred zone. A chart lists the numbers of peoples from the different countries in the world that were included in the annual quota of 100. But next to it is an asterisk with a qualification. "Quotas for the countries marked by the asterisk are intended only for persons born within those countries, who belong to races eligible to citizenship of the United States. For example: a person born in India of English parentage may be admitted, but a Hindu may not."[27]

Thus the Asians, and particularly the Asian Indians, were not affected by this legislation, as they were already declared ineligible by the earlier legislation and the Supreme Court ruling, but this Act is mentioned here to convey an idea of the prevalent racism during this period.

The Immigration Act of 1946

It was not until July 2, 1946, with the passage of Public Law 483, that Indians were officially included in the Immigration Acts. Public Law 483 was an act "to authorize the admission into the United States of persons of races indigenous to India, and persons of races indigenous to the Philippine Islands, to make them racially eligible for naturalization and other purposes.[28]

In 1946, legislation was enacted to change the immigration laws to permit Indian immigration to the United States. Public Law 483 was to amend section 303 of the Nationality Act of 1940.

The 1940 Act reads as follows:

Section 303 (a). The right to become a naturalized citizen under the provisions of this Act shall extend only to —

1. white persons, persons of African nativity or descent, and persons who are descendants of races indigenous to the Continents of North or South America, or adjacent islands and Filipino persons or persons of Filipino descent.

2. persons who possess, either singly or in combination a preponderance of blood of one or more of the classes specified in clause (1);

3. Chinese persons and persons of Chinese descent and persons of races indigenous to India; and

4. persons who possess, either singly or in combination, a preponderance of blood of one or more of the classes specified in clause (3) or, either singly or in combination, as much as one-half blood of those classes and some additional blood of one of the classes specified in clause (1).

b. Nothing in the preceding subsection shall prevent the naturalization of former citizens of the United States who are otherwise eligible for naturalization under the provisions of section 317.[29]

There was much discussion in the House of Representatives concerning this bill. In many ways it was compared to the bill allowing Chinese immigration, which was passed only a few years earlier, in 1943. In the discussion reasons both for and against the amendment were brought up.

One argument against the passage of the bill was that it would break down the principles embodied in existing immigration law. Representative McCowen of Ohio stated in opposition, "It gives a quota and breaks down a vital point in our immigration policy. It is like breaking a link in a strong, taut chain, as a result of which the entire chain falls, requiring much labor to repair and restore, even if so much damage has not been done as to make any attempt at repair or restoration impossible."[30]

According to Representative Allen of Louisiana, "For a long time now we have had in our laws this policy of excluding Asiatics. Our forefathers thought it was good. They thought it would protect American workers from cheap Asiatic labor. They evidently concluded that it was the right position for America to take. That principle has stood for a long time."[31]

Another major argument against the passage of Public Law 483 was one based on the fear that people from India could not be assimilated into American culture. Mr. Robinson of Kentucky states:

I do assert, even as some of the proponents of this bill assert, that the people of India cannot and do not assimilate with the people of the United States, and I think it is unwise from every point of view to admit peoples to this country who do not readily assimilate with the characteristics, culture, ideology, and the philosophies of government, as well as with the religion, of the people of our country.

The reason why they were excluded from the quota and from citizenship in this country was that they could not and would not assimilate readily with the American people. We know the low standards of the teeming millions of the people of India, and also their low wages, their caste system, under Indian ideals.[32]

The view of discrimination against Asians is summed up by the Representative of Connecticut, Mrs. Clare Booth Luce (in favor of the amendment):

I hope I make it clear that I would be the first to protest against people from any nation, of any color, coming here in such numbers as to lower our living standards and weaken our culture. This is a principle on which we are all agreed. And it does so happen that the peoples of the Orient can underlive us. They can live cheaper than our people will, or than the people from Germany or France or Italy will live. It does so happen that their philosophy of life and their religions are more alien to us than those of Europeans. We are utterly justified in controlling and keeping low oriental immigration in terms of numbers, because of the fact thay they in too great numbers may undermine our way of life, our living standards, our form of religion. But we are not justified in discriminating against orientals in toto, simply because they have skins of a different color. The proper reason for keeping orientals out in great numbers is because of those economic facts, but it is certainly improper to keep them out altogether, because they are orientals.[33]

The arguments supporting the passage of the bill were comparable to those which had been put forth in support of the bill allowing Chinese to come to the United States. Many stemmed from strong ties with the United States economically and politically. Not only did the Indian Army help fight as America's allies in the war; it was felt that India and China were on the verge of an industrial awakening and that the passage of the bill would help provide a market for American manufactured goods.

Some felt that allowing even a small number of Indians to immigrate to the United States would eliminate the discrimination against India. Others felt such immigration would only increase the discrimination, because of the discrepancy in the numbers of Indians in this country compared to many thousands of Germans, Englishmen, Italians, and so on. The argument in favor of the bill was based on removing the stigma of discrimination excluding the nation as a whole, by allowing a small number to apply for citizenship. Mrs. Luce stated, "If we fail to pass this bill, we shall further damage our claim to moral leadership not only throughout the Asiatic world, but here at home among our own colored people."[34]

The bill was passed on July 2, 1946. In many ways it was not an ideal piece of legislation for it contained equivocal features.

This Act authorized the admission to the United States of persons of "races" indigenous to India and to the Philippine Islands, and consequently eligible for naturalization. The quota for immigrants from India being 100 applied to all persons from India regardless of the country of their birth. Three fourths of the quota was given to Indians born and resident in India and its dependencies.

The incredibly slender beginnings of Asian Indian immigration can be seen in that only eighteen Indians were admitted under the law during the one year from the time of its enactment to June 30, 1947.

The Immigration and Nationality Act of 1952 (The McCarran-Walter Act)

The years following the Second World War witnessed several changes in the immigration laws. The Congress amended the old laws in response to altered circumstances and increasing pressures.

The 1952 Act codified all these amendments and brought together for the first time all the American legislation on immigration and naturalization. It continued and enlarged the qualitative restrictions, and continued in a revised form the unpopular national origins quota system for the selection of immigrants in effect since 1929.

In conformity with the Act's professed aim of eliminating "race" as a barrier to immigration and naturalization, the immigration regulations for Asians were liberalized. The Act set up for quota purposes a geographical area called the Asia Pacific Triangle and established, among other quotas, one for India for 100 immigrants per year. Though these were token quotas, the Asian and Pacific countries could no longer complain that their nationals could not immigrate to the United States. The quota for southern and eastern Europe was only slightly altered.

The objections to the provisions of the Bill can be seen in President Harry Truman's veto message to the House of Representatives on June 25, 1952, when he said,

> In one respect, this Bill recognizes the great international significance of our immigration and naturalization policy and takes a step to improve existing laws. All racial bars to naturalization would be removed, and at least some minimum immigration quota would be afforded to each of the free nations of Asia.
>
> The Bill would continue, practically without change, the national origins quota system which was enacted into law in 1924, and put into effect in 1^29. This quota system — always based upon assumptions at variance with our American ideals — is long since out of date and more than ever unrealistic in the face of present world conditions.
>
> The greatest vice in the present quota system, however, is that it discriminates deliberately, and intentionally, against many peoples of the world. The purpose behind it was to cut down and virtually eliminate immigration to this country from southern and eastern Europe. A theory was invented to rationalize this objective. The theory was that in order to be readily assimilable, European immigrants should be admitted in proportion to the number of persons of their respective national stocks, already here as shown by the Census of 1920. Since Americans of English, Irish and German descent were most numerous, immigrants of those three nationalities got the lion's share — more than

two-thirds — of the total quota. The remaining third was divided up among all the other nations given quotas.

> The only consequential change in the 1924 quota system which the bill would make is to extend a small quota to each of the countries of Asia. But most of the beneficial effects of this gesture are offset by other provisions of the bill. The countries of Asia are told in one breath that they shall have quotas for their nationals, and in the next, that the nationals of the other countries, if their ancestry is as much as fifty percent Asian, shall be charged to these quotas.[35]

Despite this veto message, the bill was passed. The President wanted a more liberal piece of legislation than this Act, which while liberalizing the immigration regulations for Asians, confirmed the unscientific quota system, hardened the existing barriers to immigration, and set up somewhat harsh measures to control the entry of aliens into the United States.

This act seemed to reflect, albeit indirectly, the nation's fears which led to the Internal Security Act of 1950, which barred the entry into the United States of anyone ever affiliated with a Communist or Fascist movement.

The Immigration Act of 1965

The Immigration Act of 1965 resolved the major racist features of earlier immigration. The objectives of this legislation were plainly stated by President Kennedy's message to Congress of July 23, 1963:

> The most urgent and fundamental reform I am recommending relates to the national origins quota system of selecting immigrants . . . Although the legislation I am transmitting deals with many problems which require remedial action, it concentrates attention primarily upon revision of our quota system . . . The use of a national origins system is without basis in either logic or reason. It neither satisfies a national need nor accomplishes an international purpose. In an age of interdependence among nations, such a system is an anachronism, for it discriminates among applicants for admission into the United States on the basis of the accident of

birth . . . But the legislation I am submitting will insure that progress will continue to be made toward our ideals and toward the realization of humanitarian objectives.[36]

President Lyndon B. Johnson, signing into law the 1965 Immigration Bill (H.R. 2580) in a ceremony that took place on Liberty Island in New York Harbor, flanked by Vice-President Hubert Humphrey and Senators Edward and Robert Kennedy, who actively supported the new law, said: "This is not a revolutionary bill. It does not affect the lives of millions. It will not reshape the structure of our daily lives or add importantly to our wealth and power . . . This bill says simply that from this day forth those wishing to emigrate to America shall be admitted on the basis of their skills and their close relationship to those already here."[37]

The major provisions of the Act are:

1. The national origins quota system will be abolished as of July 1, 1968. Until that time, unused visas will go into a pool and be made available to countries with long backlogs of waiting lists.

2. The bigoted Asia-Pacific Triangle provision of the Immigration Act of 1917 is repealed immediately.

3. A ceiling of 170,000 immigrant visas for Eastern Hemisphere nations exclusive of parents, spouses and children of U.S. citizens is established on a first-come, first-serve basis.

4. A ceiling of 29,000 immigrant visas annually for any one country.

5. A ceiling of 120,000 immigrant visas for natives of independent Western Hemisphere countries, exclusive of parents, spouses and children of U.S. citizens.

6. A system of seven selective preference categories are established — four of which provide for the reunion of families of U.S. citizens and resident aliens, two for professional and skilled and unskilled workers needed in the U.S., and one preference for refugees including those displaced by natural calamities.

Though Presidents Kennedy and Johnson were modest in their hopes for what the Act might achieve in accommodating the policy of the United States to the realities of the world situation and in furthering U.S. international interests, the overall numerical effect of the Act was dramatic.

The countries which had been slighted and looked down upon by implication, whether they were Asian or East European, felt that finally the U.S. had awakened to their legitimate attitudes and feelings on the question of race and national origin. No more did American rhetoric on democracy sound hollow as it had in the earlier three quarters of a century. The day had arrived when the United States gave up her long history of bigotry and prejudice on the question of immigration.

As for the number of immigrants, a new shift came into existence attempting to redress the earlier imbalance of ability and skills from hitherto unrepresented nations. The number of immigrants from such countries preferred earlier as Great Britain, Ireland and Germany decreased by more than 40 percent, and in the low quota countries it increased tremendously. For instance, for the period 1966-70 immigration from Hong Kong increased by 565 percent; from Portugal by 338 percent; and from India by 730 percent. Despite the high percentages, the absolute numbers were relatively small compared to the earlier European immigrants numbered in the millions. For the period under review, of all the immigrants, a third was from Europe, another third from Canada and Latin America, and the remaining third were from Asia, Africa and the West Indies.

While apparently the Government of India and the people of India in general welcomed this legislation, it is clear that this 1965 Immigration Law still discriminates against persons from India since the quota for India is only 20,000 out of 390,000 (5.1 percent of the total) whereas the population of India constitutes 15.3 percent of the world's population. It is obvious that in fairness to India her quota should have been considerably higher. But the U.S. might well argue that her Immigration Laws are not designed to solve the population problems of the Third World.

The 1965 Immigration Act clearly tells that the U.S. would not stringently control the future ethnic and racial composition of the American population and flatly rejected the century-old claim that some ethnic and racial groups were better suited to be Americans than others.

Two major decisions of great importance for America's relations to the entire outside world flow from this piece of legislation.

First, immigrants from every nation in the world are allowed to enter the United States. And once permitted to enter, all people have equal rights. No group would be considered superior or inferior to another.

And second, unlike in some other federal countries in the world, no group, no matter how small or new, would be asked to give up its group character and identity as the price of its acceptance into the American economic, political and social structure. This is a revolutionary departure when viewed against the century-old prejudice and discrimination, rejection and exclusiveness.

It is to America's enduring credit that, unlike many nations which have not only made profound mistakes but continue to perpetrate them, she chose to reverse her stand. As Senator Edward Kennedy, who worked hard for the enactment of this legislation, aptly points out, "A measure of greatness for any nation is its ability to recognize past errors in judgement and its willingness to reform its public policy."

If we may single out individuals, the credit for this piece of relatively progressive legislation should go to President Truman who disapproved the quota system as undemocratic and meaningless. When the Congress passed the McCarran-Walter Act President Truman vetoed it mainly because it continued the national quota system. And when the Congress passed it over his veto, he appointed a President's Commission on Immigration and Naturalization to examine all the faults and limitations of the new law. The Commission submitted its Report, *Whom We Shall Welcome* (Washington, D.C., Government Printing Office, 1953). Thus it was President Truman's Commission that really pioneered the way for the 1965 Immigration Act.

Conclusion:

The time has come for America to express in no uncertain terms her abiding belief in racial and ethnic egalitarianism as a fundamental creed for today and tomorrow, and that she does not believe "the melting pot" is really a mistake. She needs to express her belief that the melting pot contributes to the willing and voluntary fusion of all groups, and particularly the non-white peoples, into the American mainstream so that eventual physical assimilation becomes a biological and social reality. Such a process has been going on for some four hundred years slowly and imperceptibly, a little on the platform and a lot behind the curtain. Apparently a majority of the people are not against it for how else can we explain the thousands who can "pass" for "white" today. Therefore the task is to radically change the small Black and white minorities' attitudes and obscurantist racist beliefs. We cannot have a great majority's ideals of racial equality and democratic freedoms destroyed by a small minority's archaic beliefs and behavior. Naturally biological assimilation is purely a matter of personal choice. Those who make such a choice should not be denigrated in any way by those who don't. And by the same token, those who want to maintain their ethnic identity should not be denigrated for preferring to do so.

FOOTNOTES

* Professor S. Chandrasekhar is currently teaching at the University of California, Irvine, CA 92717.

1. I am indebted to Professors William Petersen and David M. Heer for their valuable suggestions in the preparation of this paper. I am also thankful to Professor Willem W. Van Groenou and Mrs. Nan Chico for providing the author with some data for this paper.

2. To distinguish the nationals of India from the Indians of North and South America, the term "East Indian" was adopted in the Americas. Columbus, when he landed in San Salvador in the Bahamas in 1492, thought he had arrived in the Indies and hence called the natives "Indians," and his mistake was perpetuated. Of course, in the rest of the world the nationals of India are simply known as Indians.

Conventionally "East Indian" was applied broadly to the peoples of the Indian sub-continent including India, Pakistan, Sri Lanka, Bangladesh, Bhutan, Sikkim, Nepal and Afghanistan.

However, "East Indian" began to be more narrowly defined to denote the people of India, Pakistan and Bangladesh, the former undivided India of British rule.

In the United States confusion became more confounded by sometimes calling the people of India "Hindus," which is as misleading as calling all the people of the United States Protestant Christians. The people of India profess many religions, all the way from Animism to Zoroastrianism, although a great majority are Hindus. The first few groups of immigrants from India to the U.S. were not Hindus but members of the Sikh persuasion.

To avoid confusion, the writer prefers the term "Asian Indians" to "East Indians" to designate the immigrants who came from India to the United States of America.

3. During the early years there were no laws or regulations governing the convenience and safety, let alone the comfort, of trans-Atlantic passengers on vessels that brought immigrants to the United States. These vessels were generally overcrowded and dirty and without sufficient food or even drinking water. To ameliorate these deplorable conditions under which immigrant passengers had to travel to reach the United States, the Congress, reflecting the humanitarian concern of the U.S. Government for the future citizens of the country, enacted a series of seven Acts. The first such Act "regulating passenger-ships and vessels" was the Passenger Act of March 2, 1819, by which a passenger ship or vessel was allowed to carry not more than two passengers for every five tons of her measurement.

A second Act, passed on February 28, 1847, allowed to each passenger "fourteen clear superficial feet of deck" if the vessel was not passing within the tropics. A third Act, of March 2, 1847, amended the earlier Act to equate two children of eight years or under as equal to one adult passenger. A fourth Act of January 31, 1848 dealt with the return of colored (black) emigrants from the U.S. to Africa, while a fifth Act, of May 17, 1848, "provided for the ventilation of passenger vessels." The sixth and seventh Acts of March 3, 1849, and March 5, 1855 amended and repealed provisions of earlier Acts and introduced new provisions — all designed to ensure certain minimum conveniences for the immigrant passengers during their travel to the U.S.

4. John Higham, "American Immigration Policy in Historical Perspective," *Law and Contemporary Problems,* Vol. 21, No. 2. Spring 1956. p. 218.

5. William Bentley, *The Diary of William Bentley,* 5 vols. (Salem: The Essex Institute, 1962) Vol. 1, p.228.

6. Walter Muir Whitehall, *The East India Marine Society and Peabody Museum of Salem* (Salem: Peabody Museum, 1852) p.34.

7. Edward Ely to Daniel Webster, 4 June 1852, Department of State, *Despatches from the United States Consuls at Bombay* (Manuscript, National Archives of the United States, Washington, D.C.)

8. R.M. Narelwala, S.M. Master, and E.J. Nehory to Secretary of State, 30 August 1876, *Despatches from the United States Consuls at Bombay* (Manuscript, National Archives of the United States, Washington, D.C.)

9. With the exception of a group of Sikhs who wanted to emigrate from their native Punjab province in India to British Columbia, Canada by S.S. Komagata Maru in 1917.

10. Dwijendranath Tripathi, "The Parsis and the United States through some unused Documents." Unpublished paper, 1980. Personal communication to the author. I am indebted to Professor Tripathi for this material.

11. Betty Lee Sung, *Mountain of Gold: The Story of the Chinese in America* (New York: Macmillan, 1967) p. 47.

12. There is a large volume of well documented literature on Chinese immigration to the United States. Only a few studies are cited here:
   Stuart C. Miller, *The Unwelcome Immigrant: The American Image of the Chinese, 1785-1882* (Berkeley, 1969)
   P. Gunther Barth, *Bitter Strength* (Cambridge, Mass., 1964)
   Elmer C. Sandmeyer, *The Anti-Chinese Movement in California* (Urbana, Ill., 1939)
   S.W. Kung, *Chinese in American Life* (Seattle, 1962)

13. The Alien Act of June 1798 was the first piece of federal legislation to deal with the expulsion of aliens from the United States. This Act, which enabled the President of the United States to deport any alien deemed dangerous to the security of the nation, expired two years after its enactment.

14. Oscar Handlin, *A Pictorial History of Immigration* (New York: Crown Publishers, 1972) p. 268.

15. Professor Maurice R. Davie writes, "Investigation, however, disclosed that proxy marriages were legal and customary in Japan and such marriages at our ports were given up. Other countries, such as Spain and Portugal and the Netherlands, permit proxy marriages. The 'importation' of wives into Virginia and California in the early days was a somewhat similar system; at least it has the same objective of increasing the number of women among a group where males were predominant. In 1933, it might be mentioned parenthetically, a man in Detroit was married by transatlantic telephone to a girl in Sweden; the latter then came to the United States where she was admitted as the wife of an immigrant resident. Nevertheless, California protested against the immigration of 'picture brides' who constituted many but not all of the 30,000 Japanese women admitted to the United States between 1908 and 1920." *World Immigration* (New York: Macmillan, 1949) p. 322-323.

The attitude of the native Californians to the arrival of wives for Asian immigrants was somewhat as follows: 1. The Asian immigrants are all single males and this leads to prostitution and vice. 2. But we are firmly opposed to these Asian males marrying local American women, and 3. We are opposed to the immigration of Asian women who could marry the Asian immigrants already here and make their lives normal family ones. (Logic!)

16. *U.S. v Bhagat Singh Thind* 261US (204-215) 1923.

17. Harold S. Jacoby, "More Thind Against Than Sinning," *The Pacific Historian,* Nov. 1958, p. 2.
The Sikh turban has a religious connotation and is not merely a secular headcovering to be doffed. Many non-Sikhs, ignorant of the Sikh religious tradition, think that Sikh men are rude in not removing their turbans, but they are not. As recently as 1971 a Sikh bus driver in Burmingham, England, was dismissed for not removing his turban while driving the public vehicle of the city municipality. But when all the Sikh workers in England threatened to strike, he was promptly reinstated.

18. As quoted in Harold S. Jacoby, op. cit. p. 2.

19. Harold S. Jacoby, Ibid, p. 2.

20. *U.S. v. Bhagat Singh* Thind 261 U.S. (204).

21. Ray E. Chase and S.G. Pandit, *An Examination of the Opinion of the Supreme Court of the United States Deciding Against the Eligibility of Hindus for Citizenship* (Los Angeles, 1926).

22. The Sutherland decision caused some sorrow and furore in India. The *Modern Review,* a responsible nationalist monthly of Calcutta, pointed out that Sutherland, an Englishman, had been born in Buckinghamshire and was himself a naturalized citizen. "It may be that he has not been able to forget his inherited predjudices against the natives of India." *Modern Review*, XXXIII, 1923.

23. For details see H. Brett Melendy, *Asians in America* (Boston: Twayne Publishers, 1977) p. 220. Also J.W. Garner, "Denationalization of American Citizens," *American Journal of International Law* XXI (1927) 106-107.

24. *United States v. Gokhale* 26 Fed. 2nd 360; *Gokhale v. United States* 278 U.S. 662.

25. As quoted in Oscar Handlin, *Race and Nationality in American Life* (Boston: Little Brown, 1957) p. 132.

26. Ronald M. Pavalko, "Racism and the New Immigration: Toward a Reinterpretation of the Experiences of White Ethnics in American Society," 1977. Unpublished paper.

27. Constantine Panunzio, *Immigration Crossroads* (New York: Macmillan, 1927) p. 147.

28. *United States Statutes at Large* (Washington, D.C.: U.S. Government Printing Offices, 1946) Vol. 1, p. 416.

29. *United States Statutes at Large*, op. cit., p. 416.

30. *Congressional Record — House,* October, 1945, p. 9525.

31. Ibid, p. 9526.

32. Ibid, p. 9539.

33. Ibid, p. 9530.

34. Ibid, p. 9528.

35. *Digest of International Law* Dept. of State Publication 8290, Sept. 1967. Vol 8, p. 585.

36. Edward M. Kennedy, "The Immigration Act of 1965," *The Annals* of the American Academy of Political and Social Science, September 1966, p. 139.

37. Edward M. Kennedy, Ibid, p. 148.

The Asian Indian Immigrants In The United States
The Early Phase, 1900-65

by

Gary R. Hess*

The considerable Indian emigration to the United States in recent years has tended to increase scholarly interest in the earlier phase of such emigration. In the first years of the twentieth century, several thousand "Hindus" entered the United States and encountered widespread hostility and discrimination. Between 1899 and 1920, some 7,300 immigrants from India, mostly agricultural laborers, arrived on the West Coast and settled mostly in California. From the beginning, the prevalent anti-Asiatic sentiment of that era led to demands for exclusion and for reduction of their political and economic rights. Ultimately, these pressures resulted in Congressional legislation which effectively ended immigration from India for three decades and a Supreme Court decision which denied citizenship to East Indians for nearly a quarter of a century. Despite this hostility, the small East Indian community endured.

The arrival of "Hindus," as South Asians were called regardless of religion, was initially a by-product of Indian emigration to Canada in the first years of the twentieth century. Most were farmers and laborers from the Punjab, where Canadian companies seeking contract labor had publicized the economic opportunities in America. Coming to British Columbia at the rate of about 2,000 per year, they quickly encountered opposition. Fear of labor competition, the seeming impossibility of assimilation, and racial antagonism led to demands for exclusion. After conferences with British and Indian authorities, the Canadian government in 1909 effectively ended Indian immigration through various means, including: (1) implementation of the "continuous voyage" provision of the Canadian immigration law, which excluded immigrants who had failed to make a single, direct voyage from their native country; (2) a reprimand of the steamship companies for misleading propaganda on economic opportunities in Cana-

da; (3) an increase in the amount of money required for immigrants to remain in the country. An important effect of the Canadian exclusion policy was to channel more Indian emigration toward the United States.[1]

Many of the immigrants looked to the United States with the highest of expectations. Writing to a popular journal in his homeland, one of the early immigrants saw the people of the world's oldest civilization under persecution in Canada, South Africa, and elsewhere coming to the world's newest civilization for asylum.[2] Such hopes, however, quickly gave way to disillusionment, for "Hindus" were immediately subject to the anti-Oriental bias prevalent in the Pacific Coast states. Anti-Indian rioting occurred in a few cities, including Seattle, Everett and Bellingham, Washington. In the most publicized incident at Bellingham in September, 1907, six hundred lumberjacks herded some two hundred "Hindus" out of town with many immigrants suffering serious injuries. A Hearst journal delighted in reporting that the "tawny subjects of Great Britain" were as docile as cattle and " . . . in one case, a schoolboy drove in three of the timorous Asiatics who had once served in the soldiery of Great Britain."[3] An hysterical article in *Overland* warned that America faced an inundation of "Hindus" since the Vedas obliged them to "cover the earth"! The Asiatic Exclusion League held the Indians responsible for the riots claiming their willingness to work for low wages and their "filthy and immodest habits" invited reprisals. Popular magazines reported that the country was experiencing a "Hindu invasion" and a "tide of turbans." H.A. Millis, chief investigator of the Immigration Commission on the Pacific Coast, studied the growing Indian community extensively in 1910. His widely publicized findings concluded that the Indians were the most undesirable of all Asiatics and the peoples of the Pacific states were unanimous in their desire for exclusion. The Asiatic Exclusion League alarmingly announced that there were over 10,000 "Hindus" in California (in fact, the total in the Pacific states was less than 6,000) and demanded relief from the Federal government. The League warned that Japanese and Italian immigration had mushroomed from similar modest beginnings.[4]

In Congress, California Representative Denver S. Church led a determined and vitriolic campaign for exclusion. Elected with the backing of the Exclusion League and pledged to its program, Church and Senator Ellison D. "Cotton Ed" Smith of South Carolina introduced measures in 1914 to exclude "Hindu" laborers. In the House of Representatives' Immigration Committee hearings, strong support came from Anthony Caminetti, Governor-General of Immigration and an official in the Native Sons of California. A speech before the House in August 1914 in which he warned that a "large percentage" of India's 350,000,000 people were anxious to bring their "superstitious and backward" culture to America typified Church's anti-Indian rhetoric; he went on to draw the following picture of Indian culture:

> Heretofore the most terrible of all the Hindu gods was the crocodile and in order to appease the wrath of these scaly and sawtoothed monsters, loving but superstitious mothers cast from the banks of the Ganges their helpless offspring into the crocodile's mouth . . . With these ideals in mind, it is plain the ideals of the Hindu will not fit the notions of the West.[5]

Although Church's demands were not initially satisfied, the exclusion of "Hindus" was accomplished in the Immigration Law passed in February, 1917 over the veto of President Woodrow Wilson. Intended primarily to restrict immigration from southern and eastern Europe, this act stipulated the literacy test requirement. It also established the "barred zone" prohibiting immigration of laborers from virtually all of Asia except Japan.

Any lingering public sympathy for the Indian immigrants was quickly dissipated by the "Hindu conspiracy." The "conspiracy" resulted from the political activities of a handful of Indian students, led by Har Dayal, who had organized the Ghadr (revolution) Party which urged the Indian immigrants living on the Coast to return home for revolutionary work to overthrow the British raj. Following his arrest as an undesirable alien and under orders to leave the United States, Dayal went to Germany where he secured backing for Ghadr activities. With the outbreak of World War I, Ghadr leaders believed that the time was opportune to launch revolutionary projects in India. In the fall of 1914, some four hundred East Indians left the United States as part of several Ghadr-organized revolutionary missions. These activities, however, failed — as a consequence of poor planning, effective British surveillance, and insufficient popular support in India. By 1917 the Ghadr movement in America had virtually collapsed. Under strong pressure from the British government, and with evidence provided by British agents, the federal government arrested 105 persons on conspiracy charges. Only thirty-five, including seventeen East Indians, were brought to trial. At the conclusion of the well-publicized trial, one of the Indian defendants — Ram Chandra — was assassinated by another Indian defendant who was immediately shot and killed by a U.S. marshal. Altogether fourteen East Indians were convicted. With the United States by the time of the trial involved in the war as England's ally, the "Hindus" thus were seen as traitors.[6]

The exclusionist campaign in California, which had ebbed somewhat during World War I, grew shortly after the war to unprecedented strength. With the backing of the American Legion, the American Federation of Labor, a variety of farm groups, and with influential journalists and politicians in the lead, the exclusionists worked to end Asian immigration completely. While the Japanese were the principal target, East Indians suffered as well. The Supreme Court's holding in the 1922 *Ozawa* decision which ruled Japanese ineligible for citizenship provided the rationale for complete exclusion, i.e. revised immigration legislation prohibiting the entry of persons ineligible for naturalization.[7]

East Indian leaders initially welcomed the *Ozawa* decision, for it seemed to confirm their claim that persons of Indian origin were entitled to United States citizenship. Since 1907 about seventy "Hindus" had been granted citizenship, although the Justice Department had consistently contested the petitions for citizenship. The lower federal courts had adhered to the precedent established in the 1910 *U.S. v. Balsara* and the 1913 re *Ahjoy Kumar Mazumdar* cases which held that Indians were Caucasians and thus qualified under the naturalization legislation of 1790 and 1875 to be considered "white persons" who were eligible for citizenship. The Supreme Court's position in the *Ozawa* decision — that "white persons" was synonymous with Caucasian — appeared to reaffirm indirectly the East Indian's claim to citizenship. Although it was possible for East Indians to find comfort in the *Ozawa* decision, it was evident that the Supreme Court justices had not considered the implications of their definition of "white persons" with respect to the established equation of East Indians with "white persons" through their identification as Caucasians.

In 1923 the Supreme Court, however, ruled that East Indians were not qualified for citizenship. In the case of *U.S. v. Bhagat Singh Thind,* the Court reasoned that the "understanding of the common man" did not associate East Indians with Caucasians. In a unanimous decision, it was argued that the term "white persons" in the naturalization statutes could not be defined simply on the basis of race (as the Court had done in the Ozawa case) but rather in accord with popular definition. Thus, the Congress of 1790 and that of 1870 assumed that the "white persons" of the naturalization statutes which they enacted referred only to Europeans. Moreover, it was maintained that the "barred zone" provision of the 1917 immigration law provided additional evidence that East Indians were not considered fit for naturalization, for in denying immigration privileges Congress had expressed implicit opposition to their naturalization. Through this process, the Supreme Court concluded that the public and Congress never intended that East Indians be given naturalization privileges; "Hindus" and their children "would retain indefinitely the clear evidence of their ancestry.[8]"

Beyond establishing the basis for denying citizenship requests of East Indians, the *Thind* decision also was used by federal authorities to annul previous grants of citizenship. Between 1923 and 1926, the naturalization of some fifty Indians was cancelled; the courts consistently upheld the government's claim that naturalization certificates had been illegally procured. Finally in 1926, a Court of Appeals hearing the case of *U.S. v Sakharam Ganesh Pandit,* denied the government's cancellation petition and upheld the argument of Pandit, who was an attorney in California, that his 1914 naturalization had been granted by a court fully authorized to do so and thus had been obtained legally. The Pandit decision slowed, but did not end the federal government's effort to revoke Indian citizenship; as late as the mid-1930s, federal authorities were still contesting naturalization certificates of East Indians.

The Thind decision subjected East Indians to additional hardships. The restrictive provisions of the California Alien Land Law prohibited the leasing or sale of land to aliens ineligible for citizenship. And the Johnson Immigration Act of 1924 denied immigration quotas to peoples who were not entitled to naturalization. (Technically India did have a quota of 100 immigrants per year, but it was used by British and other Europeans residing in India to emigrate to the United States; in the next twenty years, over 1,000 Europeans entered the United States through that means.)[9]

In the face of such pressures, many East Indians left the United States. Between 1920 and 1940, some 3,000 returned to India, most leaving voluntarily although the figure includes a few hundred deportees. By 1930, the "Hindu" population in the United States had dropped to 3,130 and, in 1940, to 2,405. During that same period, however, some 3,000 East Indians entered the United States illegally; these were mostly farm laborers who came via Mexico. Many of these men were eventually apprehended and deported, but several hundred managed to remain.

The status of the small East Indian community remained low in comparison with other groups. By 1940, only four percent held professional positions; nearly half were farm laborers and another fifteen percent had their own farms or were farm managers, while about twenty per-

cent were engaged in non-farm labor. Of the
1,600 East Indians over the age of twenty-five
more than a third had not completed one year of
schooling. The median school years completed
was 3.7 — lower than the educational level of
another racial or ethnic group reported in the
census.

It seemed to some observers that the East Indians were losing much of their cultural identity.
Due to their small numbers and patterns of
isolated living, they had difficulty forming a
strong community. The strongest unifying force
was religion, with East Indians from throughout
California (the home of sixty percent of East Indians) visiting mosques and temples on holy
days; the Sikh Temple at Stockton served as the
principal center of religious and social life for
the adherents to Sikhism, which had comprised a
large portion of the immigrants from India. Oc-
casionally, the rural East Indians found a sense
of community with the Mexican-Americans.
Owing to similarities in physical appearance and
socioeconomic status, the East Indians were frequently identified with the Mexican who generally accepted them into their community. Thus,
some of the East Indians were assimilated into
the Mexican-American subculture, a process
typically completed by marriage to Mexican
women. Through this process of "circuitous
assimilation" East Indians thus were seen as
gradually losing their own cultural identity.[10]

Despite their decreasing numbers and the opportunity for identification with the Mexican-
American community, the East Indians did
preserve much of their cultural heritage. An important factor was that East Indian men never
lost their preference for East Indian wives. And
although many did marry Americans or
Mexican-Americans, perhaps half of the men
chose to remain single, and after World War II,
when it became possible for East Indian women
to emigrate to the United States, many of the
older immigrants brought wives from India.
Had not immigration and naturalization laws
changed in 1946, the East Indian community
would almost certainly have eroded significantly
perhaps to the point of extinction.

World War II proved to be the turning point
in American naturalization and immigration
policies with respect to India. By bringing India
into greater prominence, the war produced a
movement to end the restrictive measures which
had ended East Indian immigration and denied
citizenship. After Pearl Harbor, India took on
new significance to Americans as they sought Indian cooperation in the operations against
Japan. Liberal spokesmen and some officials in
the State Department and White House looked
upon India as the crucial test of the vaguely
phrased pledge of self-determination in the
Atlantic Charter. Political developments in India
especially during the critical spring and summer
of 1942, were followed closely by the American
press, public, and government.

It was such recognition of nationalism in
China and that country's military effort which
led to the repeal of the Chinese exclusion laws
in 1943. China was granted an immigration
quota and its nationals were given naturalization privileges. A number of journalists and
Congressmen, who earlier had not been concerned with Indian immigration, soon
presented the same arguments in favor of an
identical policy for India, since it seemed obvious that independence was only a matter of
time and India was making a substantial contribution to the war effort. The movement,
however, still faced opposition from those who
believed any break in the immigraiton policy set
twenty years earlier was a dangerous precedent.

In Congress, Representatives Emanuel Celler
and Clare Boothe Luce introduced bills in
March, 1944 providing for East Indian
naturalization privileges and a quota for Indian
immigrants. An alternative measure had been
presented three months earlier by Senator
William Langer; it provided only for the granting of citizenship to all East Indians who had
entered the United States prior to 1924.
Although strongly backed by a number of
newspapers and a wide range of prominent persons including Louis Fisher, Pearl Buck,
Reinhold Neibuhr, Albert Einstein, and Roger
Baldwin, these bills all languished in committee
and died with the ending of the Seventy-Eighth
Congress.

When the Seventy-Ninth Congress convened
in January 1945, these measures were revived
and the White House gave support to the
broader Celler-Luce approach rather than the

more restrictive Langer bill. In the early months of 1945, it appeared certain that the immigration-naturalization bill would pass; on the surface opposition was minimal. With the backing of the White House and State Department and influential religious and labor groups and with the Chinese example still fresh in mind, it was anticipated that the Celler bill would be reported favorably by the House Immigration Committee. The only outspoken committee critic of the bill, Robert Ramspeck of Georgia, however, quietly rounded up backing for his position among Southern Democrats and Republicans from the Midwest. The coalition organized by Ramspeck succeeded in tabling the bill.

A few weeks later, Harry S. Truman, shortly after succeeding in becoming President, provided leadership in salvaging the Luce-Celler bill. Truman informed Samuel Dickstein, chairman of the House Immigration Committee, of his administration's support and at Celler's urging, the President met with Ramspeck and converted the Congressman from open opposition to acquiesence. This time the Immigration Committee endorsed the bill and when it was considered by the full House on October 10, supporters dominated the debate and defeated an attempt to send it back to committee. The House approved the bill by a margin of nearly three to one.

Meanwhile in the Senate, the quota and naturalization bills remained in the Immigration Committee. A subcommittee held hearings on Langer's bill in April, but had not reported favorably. Senator Richard B. Russell of Georgia, chairman of the Immigration Committee, was the principal opponent, resisting even Truman's effort to change his position.

Finally in April, 1946, a subcommittee chaired by the freshman Arkansas Senator J. William Fulbright, held hearings on the Celler bill and recommended it to the entire Immigration Committee. Russell, under pressure from Truman and colleagues on the committee, finally permitted the bill to be reported but clearly without his support. When the bill was presented to the Senate, Russell was not present and no opposition was heard. Evident in the comments from the floor in both houses, particularly the Senate, was a willingness to abandon Indian exclusion for a modest quota which would assist the United States interests in Asia. The bill was approved unanimously by the Senate on June 14, 1946. Three weeks later, Truman signed the Indian quota-immigration bill.[11]

After being excluded since 1917, natives of India had been given an annual quota of one hundred. After being denied citizenship since 1923, Indians were now eligible for United States naturalization.

The liberalization of immigration and naturalization policy facilitated an increase in the East Indian community and added immeasurably to its survival and character. Between 1947 and 1965, nearly 6,000 immigrants were admitted to the United States under the quota for India; approximately the same number were also admitted as non-quota immigrants, i.e. husbands, wives and children of American citizens. Between 1948 and 1965, a total of 1,772 persons of former Indian allegiance acquired United States citizenship.

Economically and culturally, the rural East Indians were notably strengthened in the two decades after World War II. Aided by the virtual disappearance of overt anti-Orientalism and by their typical thrift and hard-work, they tended to increase their own agricultural holdings and considerably enhanced their economic status. The Sikh heritage endured and was represented in nearly all institutionalized activities. The preference for Indian food and the speaking of Indian languages at communal gatherings also endured. While many of the immigrants after 1946 were professional men and their families, the older agrarian community was enhanced, since some of the immigrants had agrarian backgrounds and, of course, the immigration law made it possible for wives to be brought from India. Like the earlier immigrants, many of the 1947-65 arrivals came from the Punjab, and, almost without exception, married Indian women. Although the members of the East Indian community adopted American material comforts, dress, and other features of American life, they experienced slight social integration and thus retained important aspects of their own culture. To the present, the acculturation of the rural "Hindus" remains limited.[12]

FOOTNOTES

* Gary R. Hess is Professor of History and Acting Dean of Arts and Sciences, Bowling Green State University, Bowling Green, Ohio 43403.

1. S. Chandrasekhar, "Indian Immigration in America," *Far Eastern Survey* XIII (July 26, 1944), 138-43; H.A. Millis, "East Indian Immigration to the Pacific Coast," *Survey* XXVIII (June 1, 1912), 379-86; "The Hindu in America," *American Review of Reviews* XXXVII (May, 1908), 604-05.

2. Saint Nihal Singh, "Indians in America, I," *Modern Review* III (March, 1908), 204-07.

3. Werter D. Dodd, "Hindu in the Northwest," *World To-Day* XIII (November, 1907), 1157-60; Rajani Kanta Das, *Hindustani Workers on the Pacific Coast* (Berlin: Walter de Gruyter and Co., 1923), 110-12; *Outlook* LXXXVII (September 7, 1907), 7-8; *Ibid.*, (September 14, 1907), 51-52; Kalyan Kumar Banerjee, "East Indian Immigration into America; Beginnings of Indian Revolutionary Activity" *Modern Review* CXVI (November, 1964), 355-56; Elizabeth S. Kite, "An American Criticism of 'The Other Side of the Medal' — India's Freedom and World Opinion," *Modern Review* XLI (February, 1927), 168-69; "The Hindoo Question in California (A Delayed Report)," *Proceedings of the Asiatic Exclusion League* (February, 1908), 8-10.

4. *Ibid.* (January, 1910), 5-11, (March, 1910), 7-10, (April, 1910), 4-8, (September, 1910), 45-52, (October, 1910), 59-60, (January, 1911), 79-80, (March, 1911), 92; Millis, *Survey*, XXVIII, 379-86; H.A. Millis, "East Indian Immigration to British Columbia and the Pacific Coast States," *American Economic Review* I (March, 1911), 72-76; Herman Scheffauer, "The Tide of Turbans," *Forum* XLIII (June, 1910), 616-18; "The Hindu Invasion," *Colliers* XLV (March 26, 1910), 15; "The Hindu, the Newest Immigration Problem," *Survey* XXV (October 1, 1910), 2-3.

5. U.S., *Congressional Record*, 63rd Cong., 2d Sess., 1914, LI, Appendix, 842-45.

6. Kalyan Kumar Banerjee, *Indian Freedom Movement Revolutionaries in America* (Calcutta, 1969), pp. 7-21; L.P. Mathur, *Indian Revolutionary Movement in the United States of America* (Delhi, 1970), pp. 18-25; Don K. Dignan, "The Hindu Conspiracy in Anglo-American Relations during World War I," *Pacific Historical Review*, XL (1971), 56-76.

7. Roger B. Daniels, *The Politics of Prejudice: The Anti-Japanese Movement in California and the Struggle for Japanese Exclusion* (Berkeley: University of California Press, 1962), 16-102.

8. *U.S. v Bhagat Sing Thind*, 261 U.S. 204-215 (1923).

9. Taraknath Das, "Stateless Persons in the U.S.A.," *Calcutta Review* XVI (July, 1925), 40-43; James W. Garner, "Denationalization of American Citizens," *American Journal of International Law*, XXI (January, 1927), 106-07.

10. U.S. Department of Commerce, Bureau of Census, *Fifteenth Census of the U.S. 1930*, Vol. II (Washington, 1933), p. 64; U.S. Department of Commerce, Bureau of Census, *Census of the United States, 1940 — Population Characteristics of the Nonwhite Population by Race* (Washington, 1943), pp. 2-7, 17, 34, 37; Yusuf Dadabhay "Circuitous Assimilation among Rural Hindustanis in California," *Social Forces*, XXXIII (1954), 138-41.

11. Gary R. Hess, "The 'Hindu' in America: Immigration and Naturalization Policies and India, 1917-1946," *Pacific Historical Review*, XXXVIII (1969), 71-77.

12. Lawrence A. Wenzel, "The Rural Pujabis of California: A Religio-Ethnic Group," *Phylon* XXIX (1968), 245-256; Harold S. Jacoby, *A Half-Century Appraisal of East Indians in the United States* (Stockton, 1956), 10-32.

U.S. Strategies of Asian Indian Immigration Restriction 1882-1917

by

Harold S. Jacoby*

In 1886, at the time of the dedication of the Statue of Liberty in New York harbor, in a sonnet composed for the occasion, Emma Lazarus penned the lines that have become immortal among American social idealists:

> Give me your tired, your poor,
> Your huddled masses yearning to breathe free,
> The wretched refuse of your teeming shore.[1]

Attractively beautiful as these lines are, and as noble as the sentiment they seek to express may be, they reflect quite imperfectly the dominant point of view that has characterized American thinking during most of the nineteenth and twentieth centuries on the subject of immigrants from abroad — and particularly, immigrants from the countries of Asia.

Although formal federal legislation seeking to restrict immigration did not make an appearance until 1882, this date by no means marks the initial appearance of attitudes adverse toward the free movement of immigrants into the United States. For almost half a century prior to this date, attitudes and actions expressive of antagonism toward newly arrived immigrant populations had been common on the American scene. The appearance of the "Native American Party" of the 1830s and 1840s, the "Order of the United Americans," formed in New York in 1844, and the "Know-nothings" — or "American Party" — founded in 1852, all testify to the early prevalence of a dislike of immigrants, almost without regard to whatever may have been their racial or cultural antecedents.[2]

The initial legislative effort in the direction of restricting immigration, has been characterized as "selective."[3] By a series of acts extending over the period 1882 to 1917, eligibility for being accepted as an immigrant came to be dependent upon the applicant being free of certain specified mental, physical, moral, and economic disabilities.[4] Presumably, as long as the applicant — as

an individual — met these standards, he was accepted as an immigrant without regard to his — or her — country of origin, or how many other, equally qualified persons were seeking entrance from that country. That is, unless he sought to enter from one of the countries of Asia.

Pre-World War I Asian immigration came principally from three countries: China, Japan, and India. In each instance, by the time of World War I, unlimited — even selective — immigration had been brought virtually to a halt; and interestingly enough, by three different strategies.

As far as the Chinese were concerned, their immigration was at no time regulated by the policy of selective admission. In the same year — 1882 — that marked the enactment of the first selective prohibitions — those against "any convict, lunatic, (or) idiot" — a second law was passed calling for the virtual total exclusion of the Chinese. Initially enacted to be in effect for but ten years, it was extended for a second ten year period in 1892. In 1902, it was further extended, but this time with no specified terminal date.[5]

The Japanese made their first numerically significant appearance in the United States hard upon the passage of the first Chinese exclusion act, and initially were admitted under the policy of selective admission. As their numbers increased, an effort was made in 1902, in connection with the consideration of the renewal of the Chinese exclusion act, to make the law applicable to the Japanese as well as the Chinese, but neither the country nor Congress was ready for such a step.[6] Some five years later, strong sentiment had begun to build in favor of some type of exclusionary legislation, but meantime, Japan's success in the Russo-Japanese War had established her as an important world power, and President Roosevelt was reluctant to risk offending a friendly nation by any type of unilateral exclusionary action. Through diplomatic measures, he negotiated — in 1907-08 — an agreement with Japan, whereby the United States would refrain from any legislative action directed against the Japanese, and Japan, for its part agreed to discontinue the issuance of passports to members of its laboring class planning to emigrate to the United States.[7] Thus, the exclusion of this body of potential immigrants was accomplished by executive action, rather than by legislation.

Hardly had the "Gentlemen's Agreement" — between the President of the United States and the Emperor of Japan — been concluded, than elements of a third flow of immigration from Asia became evident — this time from India. In the case of the Japanese, it had taken two decades for sentiment to build in favor of their exclusion as immigrants. With the East Indians, there was no such delay. Much of the sentiment in support of Japanese exclusion had been orchestrated by the Japanese and Korean Exclusion League, formed in San Francisco in the late spring of 1905.[8] Made aware of a new "Asiatic threat," in the form of immigration from India, this organization in late 1907 changed its name to the Asiatic Exclusion League, and widened its focus of attention to include the anticipated flood of immigration from India.[9]

Using as a model the manner in which Chinese immigration had been "managed," the League and other opponents of East Indian — usually referred to as "Hindu" — immigration, took steps aimed at securing exclusionary legislation. In 1908, the League reported that Senator Frank Flint of California was planning to introduce such a measure, but there is no record that he actually did so.[10] Thereafter, however — and with some regularity — bills embodying a variety of proposals designed to restrict or prohibit East Indian immigration, were introduced into Congress, few of which were heard from after their introduction. The House Committee on Immigration in 1914 went so far as to hold formal hearings on three measures that had been introduced respectively by Congressmen Raker and Church of California, and Humphrey of Washington, but the hearings attracted only a limited amount of interest, and none of the bills

was reported out by the Committee.[11] It was evident that because the concern about this new immigration arose from an — as yet — insignificant number of new arrivals, and was a situation confined almost exclusively to the Pacific coast, the issue was not one on which Congress was prepared to act. But if Congress was unimpressed with the need for restrictive action, there was another branch of government that thought otherwise, and was prepared to take action — the Bureau of Immigration and Naturalization.

Looked at from the standpoint of theory, one might have expected the Bureau to serve merely as an objective and impartial agency for the administration of statutory law, but in practice it proved to have been an active and enthusiastic participant in the total effort to minimize East Indian immigration. Having through the years come to accept the philosophy upon which the emerging immigration law was based, the Bureau saw itself as the guardian of the outer ramparts, charged with the responsibility for initiating defensive measures against new immigration threats until they could properly be dealt with through legislative action.

Considering the leadership which the Bureau enjoyed, it is no mystery how this wider conception of its role came into being. From 1902 to 1908, the Commissioner General of the Bureau was Frank P. Sargent, who from 1885-1902 had been Chief of the Brotherhood of Locomotive Firemen. He was followed until 1913, by Daniel J. Keefe, a one-time vice-president of the American Federation of Labor, and for fifteen years President of the Longshoreman's Association. In view of the role of organized labor in the formation of the United States' immigration policy, it need not be wondered at that at times the Bureau's enforcement of the law went above and beyond the call of impartial interpretation. Nor was Keefe's successor under the Wilson administration one whit less devoted to the same point of view. A veteran legislator in California, Anthony Caminetti had also served two terms in the House of Representatives prior to his appointment. Of more specific significance, he was an active leader in the Native Sons of the Golden West, a civic organization in California that had taken a strong stand in support of the total exclusion of all orientals, and was personally committed to this point of view. In the course of the 1914 Congressional hearings, Caminetti had testified:

> I came from the Pacific coast, where we have had two race problems which we have had to fight, and the third one about to be thrown upon us out there . . . The people of California waited very patiently for diplomatic arrangements upon the Japanese immigration problem . . . and I do not think they are anxious now for diplomatic arrangements upon the Hindu problem. That is my individual opinion.[12]

The manner of operation of the Bureau was simple and direct. Charged with the responsibility of assessing the eligiblity of each prospective immigrant, the Bureau quite early undertook the stringent scrutiny of each applicant, looking toward the disqualification of as many of them as possible. Nor was this at all a covert or unacknowledged operation. The following, from the 1910 report of the District Commissioner of Immigration at Seattle may not have reflected perfectly the accomplishments at the other ports of entry, but it reveals quite openly the spirit of the Bureau's operation:

> A number of Hindus have applied for admission to the United States through this district during the year just passed. Every Hindu has been rejected by a board of special inquiry on the ground of belief in polygamy, likely to become a public charge, doctor's certificate, or as an assisted immigrant.[13]

Such a policy, of course, had a two-fold effect. Not only did it succeed in reducing the number of arrivals who were admitted, but knowledge of its existence undoubtedly served to discourage a number already planning to book passage to the United States. Just how effective these influences were during the years prior to World War I is reflected in Table A, which summarizes by year the percentage of East Indians who presented themselves for admission but were debarred from entering the country. As indicated in this table, once the Bureau had become alerted to the rise in the number of applicants — as occurred following 1906 — its restrictive efforts began to show results, and while

they never became one hundred percent effective, for several years, half or more of the would-be immigrants were turned back.

TABLE I

Annual number and percentage of East Indians debarred from entering the United States at ports of entry, 1906-1915.*

Year	East Indians Seeking Admission	East Indians Debarred	
		Number	Percentage
1906	295	24	8
1907	1489	417	28
1908	2148	438	20
1909	668	331	50
1910	2193	411	19
1911	1378	862	63
1912	269	104	39
1913	424	236	56
1914	332	160	48
1915	386	304	79

*Compiled by writer from *Annual Reports,* 1910-1915.

Initially, a high proportion of the rejections were based on physical reasons — physical defects or alleged presence of some "contagious disease," but rather quickly pre-embarkation physical examinations were set up in Asian ports by steamship companies and even by groups of prospective immigrants themselves, to screen out possible rejectees; and this reduced the number arriving at American ports with significant health problems. In 1908, seventy percent of the rejections were for health reasons. The next year, the percentage dropped to forty-four; but more importantly the numbers presenting themselves for admission declined from 2148 to less than 700 — circumstances undoubtedly related to the stringency of the pre-embarkation examinations. As the health level of the applicants improved, however, it was not difficult for the Bureau to find other reasons for debarring. Since many of the arrivals were of the Muslim faith, they were vulnerable to the charge of believing in the practice of polygamy . But the most frequently used basis for exclusion as time went on was that of being "likely to become a public charge." Few of the arrivals were wealthy, and without evidence of promised employment — which would have brought them under the ban as being "assisted" immigrants — it was comparatively simple to exclude them on economic grounds. Even in those instances in which an applicant had some funds, it was possible for the Bureau to deny admission by the expedient of citing the widespread existence of prejudice in west coast communities which — allegedly — would make it difficult for the immigrant to secure employment, thus leading to his becoming a public charge. At one hearing, affidavits were presented on behalf of a group of newly arrived East Indians,

> denying the existence of prejudice against people of that race . . . (and offering) employment to the aliens under arrest should they be permitted to remain in the country.[14]

But the Bureau held doggedly to its contention, and refused to reconsider its original decision. Over the years 1907 through 1915, this public charge provision, together with the health requirement, accounted for well over ninety percent of all exclusions.[15]

As the Bureau's efforts became more effective, the East Indians sought to circumvent them by the expedient of first gaining entrance to the Hawaiian or Philippine Islands, and then entering the United States from these points. Under a Bureau regulation known as Rule 14, any alien admitted to one of the island possessions of the United States was eligible to enter the mainland merely on the presentation of an appropriate certificate issued by the island authorities.

Technically, the same entrance regulations applied to the islands as to the mainland, but because the administration of the regulations in the islands was in the hands of the Bureau of Customs rather than the Bureau of Immigration and Naturalization, differences occurred in the interpetation of the laws. For one thing, the Customs officials were not so strongly indoctrinated with anti-Asian sentiment as were the immigration authorities, and hence were more likely to administer the law with some measure of impartiality. Secondly, island conditions in certain respects provided quite different circumstances than were presented by the mainland, particularly as they affected the likelihood of the applicants becoming public charges.[16]

Although this practice was publicly commented upon as early as 1910,[17] the first mention of it by the Bureau was contained in the 1913 Report of the District Commissioner of Immigration from San Francisco:

> Late in the fiscal year . . . a few Hindus arrived from Manila, P.I., and . . . it was disclosed that the service was soon to be confronted with a systematic effort . . .to make the Philippines a "back door" entrance to the mainland of the United States. Steps were being taken as the year closed.[18]

The steps referred to consisted of amending Rule 14 to permit the review of all certificate holders with respect to the likelihood of their becoming charges, an action which the Bureau took on June 16, 1913. Commenting on this action a year later, the District Commissioner of Immigration for Seattle wrote:

> The present administration, very wisely, we think, regarded their entry to the islands as a mere subterfuge, and promulgated the present rules, which have resulted in stopping their migration for the time being.[19]

Meanwhile, the Bureau had resorted to still another defensive tactic. Early in the summer of 1913, conversations were held with the major steamship companies serving the trans-Pacific trade, requesting their cooperation in terminating the flow of applicants from India. These conversations, apparently, had the desired effect. In 1914, the District Commission of Immigration at Seattle reported that

> the steamship companies entering this district have agreed to carry no more Hindu laborers for the present.[20]

And Comissioner General Caminetti was able to declare that

> since last summer we have had practically a cessation of this immigration.[21]

All indications, nevertheless, point to the conclusion that the Bureau — and its supporters — were nervous about the future. The arrangements with the steamship companies they recognized, were only stop-gap measures, agreed to by the companies because they had been led to believe that Congress would soon pass a total exclusion law.[22] The East Indians, meanwhile, where beginning to acquire friends among the

American population, who were willing to assist them in appealing the rulings of the Bureau to the courts. As reported by a Portland (Ore.) immigration official in 1915:

> This office has caused the arrest of several Hindus on a charge of entry without inspection. On such occasions it invariably has met with extraordinary opposition by the defense. Release on bond is promptly had, and the best legal talent available is retained to resist the Government's action.[23]

Nor were the courts always as supportive as the Bureau felt they should be. Complained a San Francisco official in the same year:

> Although the court's favorable rulings in the (Hindu) cases that have been discussed in the foregoing . . . have given this office no little inspiration in its difficult task of enforcing the immigration . . . laws, its unfavorable rulings in other cases, in which it has criticized the department and us, have sometimes had a correspondingly depressing effect.[24]

Faced with these uncertainties with respect to its ability to "hold the line," the Bureau felt impelled to stress the need for legislation:

> The safest plan (wrote an immigration official in 1914) to preclude the possibility of a Hindu invasion is for Congress to enact a suitable exclusion law.[25]

The outbreak of World War I in August presented the Bureau with two favorable developments. It occasioned an interruption in the flow of applicants for admission, and it triggered a reverse flow of several hundred militantly anti-British East Indians — chiefly Sikhs — who left the United States for India to take part in a rebellion that never took place.[26] All indications are that the 1917 population of East Indians in the United States was ten percent less than it had been in 1912.[27] The Bureau, however, was not to be content with this type of temporary circumstance, and it continued its advocacy of statutory relief — which came in the Immigration Law of 1917.

It is unlikely that the relief the Bureau sought would have come as quickly — if at all — had it not been for the convergence of the interests of eastern and western legislators in the matter of immigration. For several years, eastern and middle western groups had sought to require a literacy test for persons seeking admission as immigrants, but twice measures embodying this requirement had been met with presidential vetoes — by Taft in 1913, and by Wilson in 1915.[28] In both instances, efforts had been made to override the veto, but without success. Determined to make another effort, Congress in 1916 decided to undertake a total revision of the immigration law, and incorporate in the revision the controversial literacy test provision.

Immediately, a number of western senators, aware that their support would be crucial not merely to the passage of the legislation, but to the overriding of the anticipated veto, pressed for the inclusion of some type of ban on immigration from Asian countries in the projected revision. Initially, they supported a proposal to name the countries from which immigrants would not be welcome, but fearing that such use of specific names might give offense to otherwise friendly countries, other congressional leaders proposed accomplishing the same objective by establishing a "barred zone," delineating by parallels of latitude and meridians of longitude an area of Asia and of the Pacific and Indian Oceans, the nationals of which would be ineligible for admission as immigrants. Without naming countries, the proposed zone effectively included all of India, Indo-China, and the East Indies, and most of China and Afghanistan. By appropriate wording, Japan and the Philippines were exempted from the provisions of the law, the former because it was a party to the "Gentlemen's Agreement," and the latter because it was a possession of the United States. By January, 1917, the completed revision of the immigration law had been approved by both houses of Congress.

Because the legislation contained the literacy test provision, President Wilson, as he had promised, vetoed the bill. This time, however, both houses had strength enough to override the veto, and in February the measure became law.[29] Besides the literacy test requirement, the United States now had a statutory basis for the control of East Indian immigration, ending almost a decade of control by bureaucratic policy making and administration.

Several years later — in 1924 — in another revision of the immigration law, all of the existing strategies of restriction relative to Asian populations were set aside in favor of a uniform and wholly new approach. It having been determined in a series of court actions that neither the Chinese, the Japanese, or the East Indians were eligible for naturalization under the laws of the United States,[30] the new immigration law bluntly declared that henceforth "no alien ineligible to citizenship shall be admitted to the United States," a regulation which remained in effect until 1952.

FOOTNOTES

* Professor of Sociology, Emeritus; University of the Pacific, Stockton, California 95211.

1. "The New Colossus" in *The Women Poets in English: An Anthology,* Ann Stanford, ed. (New York: McGraw-Hill, 1972), p. 141.

2. Maurice R. Davie, *World Immigration* (New York: Macmillan, 1936), pp. 84-92.

3. *Ibid.,* p. 369.

4. For list of specific disabilities, see: *Ibid.,* pp. 387-89.

5. The Three Chinese Exclusion Acts: 22 Stat. 58 (1882); 27 Stat. 25 (1892); 32 Stat. 176 (1902).

6. Roger Daniels, *The Politics of Prejudice* (New York: Atheneum, 1968), pp. 21-23.

7. Davie, op. cit., pp. 321-22.

8. *San Francisco Chronicle,* 8 May 1905; *Proceedings of the Asiatic Exclusion League* (San Francisco: January 1908), p. 19.

9. The first use of the new name appears in the December 1907 issue of the *Proceedings.*

10. *Proceedings,* op. cit., 1908.

11. U.S. Congress, House, Committee of Immigration, *Hearings on Hindu Immigration,* 63 Cong., 2nd sess. 1914. (Hereafter referred to as: *Hearings.*)

12. *Ibid.,* p. 44.

13. U.S. Department of Commerce and Labor, *Reports.* "Annual Report of the Commissioner General of Immigration." 1910. p. 302.

14. U.S., Department of Labor, Bureau of Immigration, *Annual Report of the Commissioner General of Immigration,* 1914, p. 321.

15. Compiled from the *Annual Reports of the Commissioner General of Immigration,* 1910 through 1915.

16. Commissioner General Caminetti in 1914: "I want to be understood as saying the Bureau is not administering the immigration law (in the Islands). It is being administered there by other departments of the Government; hence they are not carrying out the rules as we carry them out on the mainland; and they were looser in their administration and not as particular. *Hearings,* 1914, p. 136.

17. *Proceedings,* Oct. 1910. Inasmuch as on 8 March 1905, the *San Francisco Chronicle* was protesting against the use of the Hawaiian Islands as a "half-way-house" by the Japanese, this practice by the East Indians need not have taken the Bureau by surprise.

18. *Annual Report,* 1913, p. 240.

19. *Annual Report,* 1914, p. 305.

20. *Ibid.,* p. 306.

21. *Hearings,* p. 49.

22. *Ibid.,* p. 50.

23. *Annual Report,* 1914, p. 315.

24. *Ibid.,* p. 322.

25. Ibid., p. 306.

26. Kalyan Kumar Banerjee, *Indian Freedom Movement Revolutionaries in America* (Calcutta: Jijnasa, 1969), pp. 29-39. See also: Laxman Prasad Mathur, *Indian Revolutionary Movement in the United States of America* (Delhi: S. Chand & Co., 1970).

27. Based on detailed calculations made by the writer.

28. *New York Times:* 15 February, 1913; 29 January 1915.

29. Act of February 5, 1917. 39 Stat. 874.

30. Chinese: In re Gee Hop, 71 F. 274 (1895); U.S. v. Wong Kim Ark, 169 U.S. 649 (1898). Japanese: In re Saito, 62 F. 126 (1894); Ozawa v. U.S. 260 U.S. 178 (1922). East Indians: U.S. v. Bhagat Singh Thind 261 U.S. 204 (1923).

Revolution in India: Made in America

by

Emily C. Brown*

It may seem a stretch of imagination to associate an attempt at armed revolution in India with the immigration policy of the United States, but this was precisely the case.

From the very beginning — meaning the year after the Constitution of the United States was promulgated — immigration policy was based on racial distinctions. In 1790, Congress passed a law limiting naturalization to "free white persons." This bill was amended in 1870 to extend naturalization to include "aliens of African nativity or persons of African descent." It was assumed that only those eligible for citizenship would come to America, so this would automatically limit immigration: a false assumption. Asians had to be dealt with.

By 1880, there were 75,000 Chinese in California (comprising nine percent of the population of that state) who were considered a threat both to American labor and to the American way of life and system of values: "The fundamental objection to the Orientals," said Thomas A. Bailey, with a touch of irony, "was not that they were inefficient but that they were too efficient."[1] In any case, the Americans felt that something had to be done. In 1882, the Chinese Exclusion Act was passed, marking the first attempt by Congress to regulate immigration. At the same time, an interesting new facet was introduced with provision being made for deportation of those who might be considered undesireable aliens. This later proved to be the only constraint that could be used against the Indians.

Subsequent legislation made restrictions more stringent so that by the end of the 19th Century the "Chinks" had been dealt with; but the "Yellow Peril" persisted with the influx of the Japanese. This was handled by what is known as a "Gentleman's Agreement," negotiated in 1907 by diplomatic notes. The Japanese government bound itself to issue no more passports to Japanese laborers — coolies — who wanted to come to the United States.

The Asiatic Exclusion League, a vociferous California organization, and the American Federation of Labor, which had both worked so tirelessly for the control of the immigration of "slants," now breathed a sigh of relief and began to dismantle their propaganda machines — but not for long.

There had appeared on the Pacific Coast another "menace," another tide to be stemmed. This time, it was the so-called "Tide of Turbans," the Hindus, or the "ragheads," as they were more inelegantly termed. Hindu, by the way, was the generic term used for all those who came from India, including Moslems, Sikhs, and even Christians. This was in order that East Indians not be confused with American Indians.

ASIAN INDIAN IMMIGRATION INTO THE UNITED STATES 1899-1913[2]

Year	Admitted	Debarred	Deported
1899	15	0	0
1900	9	0	0
1901	20	1	0
1902	84	0	0
1903	83	0	1
1904	258	7	2
1905	145	13	0
1906	271	24	2
1907	1072	417	0
1908	1710	438	9
1909	337	331	1
1910	1782	411	4
1911	517	862	36
1912	165	104	11
1913	188	236	32
	6656	2844	98

The arrival of the Indians in America posed problems not previously confronted by the

United States Bureau of Immigration because there existed no legislation or executive agreements under which they could act to control their coming. While the actual number of Indians arriving in the United States was relatively small, the fact that arrivals were increasing in such dramatic proportion was causing concern. As the statistics prepared by the Department of Labor indicate, almost five times more Indians arrived in 1907 than had come in 1906; in 1908, there were even more.

Indians were debarred from entry into the United States on the basis of the following: "likely to become a public charge; surgeon's certificate of mental or physical defect which may affect alien's ability to earn a living; dangerous disease, notably trachoma; contract labor; polygamy; geographically excluded, and other." Under the last-named category, only four Indians were excluded in the period 1907-1920.[3]

Although the number of Indians debarred from entry into the United States increased significantly in 1907 and 1908, It was not until 1909 that there was a marked decrease in the number of immigrants. American officials felt that their rigid screening had done its work but then, in 1910, came more Indians than ever before, giving rise to increased agitation.

The Asiatic Exclusion League, which had been lulled into relative quietude by governmental steps taken to curtail immigration from China and Japan, began to give tongue, as did other organizations on the West Coast, and the baying was heard in Washington.[4] During 1910, three influential magazines having wide readership called attention to the rising immigration figures. *Collier's* called it a "Hindu invasion" which was beginning to assume "alarming proportions." Many people, it said, did not approve of the tactics and extreme pronouncements of the Asiatic Exclusion League but, nonetheless, popular sentiment — in California, at any rate — was behind the League's appeal to the Capitol. According to *Colliers's,* the only thing that the Indians had in common with the Americans was a desire for money.[5] The theme of assimilation was taken up by *The Survey* and a San Francisco minister was quoted as saying that the habits of the Hindus, "their intense caste feeling, their lack of home life — no women being among them — and their effect

upon standards of labor and wages, all combine to raise a serious question as to whether the doors should be kept open or closed against this strange, new stream."[6] But *Forum* raised the crucial issue with the observation that "No legal bar, under the present treaty, can be set up against the coming of Hindoos. Being subjects of Great Britain, they possess an undisputed right of entry to the United States."[7]

The United States was thus faced with a delicate problem. The only weapon available was refusal of entry. Joan M. Jensen in her study on American immigration policy towards East Indians, points out that American officials were forced to develop a "legal theory" to support its debarment practices. This theory, she says, was based on the assumption that there was an existing public prejudice against East Indians which would lead to lack of employment and, without employment, the alien would become a public charge.[8]

Although this was a "particularly ingenious" theory which eventually led to debarment for many Indians, those already in the United States were far from being public charges. In Washington and Oregon they were employed in the lumber mills and, in California, in agriculture. They were not considered as industrious as the Chinese and were characterized as "doing the least work and requiring the most supervision," but they would accept extremely low wages and were thus employable.[9] Some had amassed substantial wealth and farmed independently and almost all were able to put by savings, which were usually remitted to India. This was because they lived frugally and spent very little on food, clothing, housing, or entertainment.

The overwhelming majority of the Indians in the United States, despite their labeling by the U.S. Department of Labor as Hindus, were Sikhs.[10] They came primarily from the Punjab, where, for the most part, they had been agriculturists. A significant number of them were also veterans of military service with the British. Indications are that those who had served in China during the Boxer Rebellion heard of the riches to be gained on the American continent and had first been attracted to Canada. From there, they filtered into the United States, where they found the climate — political as well as meteorological — more salubrious. They sent back word to their friends at home and soon Sikhs began coming directly to the United States in, as has been indicated, increasingly greater numbers.

The Sikhs were at somewhat of a loss as to how to cope with tightening immigration restrictions. They were organized through their *Khalsa* (the Sikh congregation or community) and had leadership in their *Diwan* (governing body) and they maintained relationships through their network of temples, but they did not know to whom to turn for redress in the United States. Khushwant Singh, who has written a history of the Sikhs, points out that the only method known to them for redress of their grievances was to work through Constitutional channels in their homeland. Since many of them were ex-soldiers or policemen, says Singh, "their loyalty to the British Crown was an article of faith." When petitions, memoranda, and pleading by delegates failed to achieve results, he points out, "they were persuaded to lend an ear to more radical counsel." This radical counsel came from those who could properly be classified as Hindus, notably a fellow Punjabi known as Har Dayal, who had established quite a reputation for himself as an extremist nationalist in Europe as well as in India. Moreover, he was the darling of Bay Area radicals and liberals and had contacts on both the Stanford and Berkeley campuses. A master propagandist who attracted publicity to himself and whatever causes he espoused, he was "able to persuade the immigrants to give up appealing to Christian sentiment and sending petitions to the English royal family, viceroys, prime ministers, and governors."[11]

Under Har Dayal's leadership they organized on a patently more activist basis through the Hindu Association of the Pacific Coast, which came into being towards the end of May, 1913.[12] It was an uneasy coalition between Hindu intellectuals and Sikh farmers, peasants, and mill workers but out of it came a movement which was to dumfound the British and discomfit the Americans who, themselves, had risen against the British to attain their own independence.

The Hindu Association of the Pacific Coast was a widespead organization with unlimited membership. Its primary function was to provide a mailing list for the free distribution of revolutionary material and to raise funds for the support of publishing activities. Publishing activities, however, were in the hands of members of an inner group called the Ghadr Party. Ghadr is a Hindi word meaning "mutiny." The Party was headquartered in San Francisco at what was called the Yugantar (meaning "new era") Ashram to which only the elect and select of the Party were admitted.

The culmination of Har Dayal's organizational activities on the West Coast was marked by the appearance of the Party's newspaper, also called *Ghadr*[13] and which was to carry the revolutionary message to India via the Sikhs, who were urged to forward copies to their friends and relations at home. The motto carried on the masthead was "O, people of India, arise and take up your swords!" and Har Dayal wrote in the leading editorial, "Our name and work are identical." Mutiny, he said, would break out in India and preparations were to be made for the rising.

This first issue of *Ghadr* and all that succeeded damned British rule in all of its aspects. The central theme was that the British were behind every disabililty suffered by every Indian, even in the United States. Go for the jugular. If India were a free sovereign nation it could protect its citizens and speak for them in Washington. Nobody seemed to notice that the free and sovereign nations of China and Japan had not had much luck in easing immigration restrictions against their citizens. If anything, the Indians were better off than either the Chinese or Japanese as they were not yet totally excluded. But revolution had a more ringing sound than reason.

The British were actually not concerned with restrictions imposed on Indians wishing to come to the United States but they were concerned with the agitation to which these restrictions had given rise, especially as the international situation worsened. The first issue of *Ghadr* had appeared in November of 1913 and the sound of cannon was to be heard in August of 1914.

Leaders of the Ghadr movement were well aware of the international tensions and were quick to recognize that Germany was a power likely to be friendly to India's nationalistic aims. At a Ghadr-sponsored rally of Indians held in Sacramento on December 31, 1913, the San Francisco German Consul General was a special guest. Har Dayal, the principal speaker, was reported by British agents to have said that "Germany was preparing to go to war with England, and that it was time to get ready for the revolution."[14] It was obvious that the British were closely monitoring Ghadr activities and they were immeasureably helped by informers in the Ghadr ranks.

British interference was notable in the case of Har Dayal and it is pretty well documented[15] that United States immigration officials arrested Har Dayal and started deportation proceedings.[16] He had brought himself forcibly to the attention of high U.S. and British officials when he appeared in Washington in February of 1914 as a member of a delegation of Indians who had come to protest at hearings on Congressional bills which would exclude immigration of all Asians to the United States. The Indians were arguing that they could not be excluded racially because they were of Aryan (Caucasian) stock and that they were not likely to become public charges. The delegation was given short shrift, with publicity being focused on the remarks of the Commissioner-General of Immigration (himself a Californian) who said that statistics indicating that there were only 6,656 in the United States were "fallacious and misleading. There are at least 30,000 Hindus in California alone and many in the states of Oregon and Washington."[17] Many Americans felt that they had reason for genuine alarm.

Meanwhile, Ghadr continued its diatribe against the British and capitalized on a situation in Canada to issue a call to arms. The Canadians had progressively tightened immigration controls. One of their stipulations was that all immigrants must come by continuous journey from the countries of their birth or citizenship. They had also imposed an embargo on the entry of all Indian laborers into Canada. Gurdit Singh, a wealthy Sikh trader from Singapore, decided to challenge the Canadian restrictions. Accordingly, he formed a navigation company in Hong Kong and chartered a Japanese ship, the *Komagata Maru,* and loaded it with a total of 376 passengers, overwhelmingly Sikhs. The ship arrived in Vancouver on May 23, 1914, and was not brought into the docks for fear the passengers might jump ship. For two months it was anchored in the roads while Gurdit Singh

tried unsuccessfully to land his people. When the Japanese captain of the ship told harbor officials that he was preparing to depart, the Indian passengers took control of the ship in a virtual mutiny.

In the early morning hours of the following day, a sea-going tug set out for the ship with 120 policemen and 40 special immigration officials aboard. The tug, which rode 15 feet lower than the *Komagata Maru,* made a serious tactical mistake by tying up to the steamer with a grappling hook. The Indians — many of them battle-seasoned veterans — were ready. They successfully defended the *Komagata Maru* with a fusillade which included lumps of coal, bricks, pieces of scrap metal, and chunks of concrete out of the boiler seatings. They had also made clubs for themselves, and spears, which they launched with careful aim. Forty injured lay on the decks of the battered tug, its superstructure virtually dismantled. It was a victory for the Indians, but only a temporary one. The Canadians called in the navy to form a picket around the steamer and held it at bay until the officers regained control and it was able to sail four days after the assault.[18]

While the *Komagata Maru* was on the high seas on its return trip, the European war broke out. In San Francisco, *Ghadr* began the clarion call for mobilization. Its editors seized upon the naval victory at Vancouver to insist that Indians return to their homeland and continue the battle. The trumpet of war was sounded with the following lines, heavily underscored:

> Enough: Wake, O Hindus and rub your eyes. Open your minds. Store your wealth in the *Ghadr* office and register your name in the army of the Ghadr. Cleanse your blood. How long will you remain seated in lethargy? Be ready to spring like tigers.[19]

In the following week's issue, there appeared an advertisement, perhaps the most quoted of the *Ghadr* pronouncements:

WANTED

Fearless, courageous soldiers for spreading mutiny in India

Salary: Death
Reward: Martyrdom and Freedom
Place: The Field of India[20]

British intelligence estimated that more than 8,000 Indians in Canada, the United States, the Philippines, Hong Kong and China heard the call and hastened to their homeland.[21] Most were taken into custody as soon as they arrived at an Indian port and were either imprisoned or returned to their villages under surveillance and warned not to participate in any political activity. Most heeded the warnings. Enough filtered through to form the nucleus of a revolutionary " army".

The grand strategy called for suborning Indian troops serving the British, notably the Sikh regiments. They were to mutiny and drive the British out while villagers were to unite and carry out harassing action. This would be the time to strike, it was reasoned, with the British occupied on the European battlefields with Germany as an ally. Efforts were actually made to land German-bought arms on India's shores but one German-financed plot after another failed because of either compromise or bungling.

In Berlin, an Indian Committee of National Independence had been formed and Har Dayal surfaced as a member. He, and others like him, thought that the Germans would support armed revolution in India via Afghanistan and were disillusioned to discover that their main interest was in Turkey and the Berlin-Bagdad railroad. Bickering and backbiting hampered the activities of the Berlin Committee, which knew little of what was going on elsewhere.

In the Punjab, February 21 had been set as the date for revolution to begin with simultaneous eruptions of violence taking place in the towns and cantonments of the Indo-Gangetic plain from Lahore to Calcutta. But nothing happened. Two days before the planned uprisings, the British moved into the revolutionaries' headquarters and took most of the leaders into custody. Some escaped and carried on sporadic harassing action and it took almost six months for the British to bring the abortive revolution under control. Twelve special tribunals were held and 175 revolutionaries were put on trial. Of this number, 136 were convicted: 18 were hanged; 58 were transported for life, and the remainder were given less severe sentences. The "revolution" was over.[22]

Ghadr activities in India and the German connection were brought to the attention of the American public when the trials in India were reported in an American newsmagazine.[23] After the United States entered the war, the American government held its own "conspiracy" trial in San Francisco.[24] Eight Germans, seven Americans and 14 Indians were convicted. Sentences ranged from two years to four months imprisonment in either the San Francisco jail or a federal institution.

The Americans, in the meantime, had moved to cut off any further immigration of Indians. In February of 1914, on the eve of the U.S. entry into World War I, a new immigration bill was passed over the veto of Woodrow Wilson. This bill included what is known as the "barred zone" provision. A line was drawn from the Red Sea to the Mediterranean Sea, Agean Sea, Sea of Mamora, Black Sea, Caucasus Mountains, Caspian Sea, Ural River, and Ural Mountains and persons born east of this line (except for Turks and those aliens regulated by existing agreements, meaning the Japanese) were barred from entry into the United States. The bill also included literacy requirements.

Although Indians protested, they were unable to challenge the legislation which successfully excluded any further immigration. Indians already here who had managed to be naturalized suffered a severe blow in 1923 when the Supreme Court argued that Congress intended that those from the barred zone were to be excluded from naturalization as well as immigration. The racial issue was once again raised and the Court ruled that Indians might well be Caucasians but could not be considered "white" in the common man's understanding of the term, "white person." Not only were further naturalizations halted but cancellation proceedings were initiated against Indians already naturalized. Such retroactive cancellations were finally halted by court action in 1928 but the Indians in the United States were forced to pass through two uneasy decades until, in 1946, a bill was passed eliminating all racial qualifications for naturalization, thus opening the way for Indians already in the United States to become citizens. This, however, did not help those whose naturalizations had been cancelled; they had to go through the process all over again.

When India became independent, Indians

were placed on an equal footing with other aliens, in terms of both immigration and naturalization.

It is doubtful whether Indian political activity — the Ghadr movement — had any effect on American immigration policy but there is little doubt of the reverse of the proposition. The British felt the fury as the proponents of revolution had predicted. Unfortunately, there was a tragic backlash. A Ghadrite, convicted in the San Francisco conspiracy case, pointed out that the Amritsar Massacre of 1919 could be traced to the Ghadr movement: "The British fired because they had been frightened by our propaganda written in San Francisco. If we had achieved that much, to make those idiots believe, then we had done something. They took us seriously, so seriously that they blew our heads off."[25]

FOOTNOTES

* Emily Brown, Ph.D., Visiting Scholar, University of Arizona, Tucson, Arizona 85721.

1. Thomas A. Bailey, *A Diplomatic History of the American People,* 4th ed. (New York: Appleton-Century-Crofts, Inc., 1950), p. 428.

2. Memorandum regarding Hindu Migration to the United States, January 23, 1914. Records of the Bureau of Immigration of the Department of Labor, National Archives, Record Group 85.

3. For a breakdown, see Rajani Kanta Das, *Hindustani Workers on the Pacific Coast* (Berlin: Walter De Gruyter & Co., 1923), Table VIII.

4. "The Hindu: The Filth of Asia," *The White Man,* August, 1910 (Publication of the Asiatic Exclusion League, San Francisco).

5. "Hindu Invasion," *Collier's National Weekly,* March 26, 1910, p. 15.

6. "The Hindu — The Newest Immigration Problem," *The Survey,* October 1, 1910, p.2.

7. Herman Scheffauer, "Tide of Turbans," *Forum,* XLIII (June, 1910), 616.

8. Joan M. Jensen, "The Great White Wall: East Indian and American Immigration Policy 1900-1946," paper presented at the Sympomsium on East Indian Immigration, Center for South and Southeast Asia Studies, University of California, Berkeley, June 23, 1979.

9. H.A. Millis, "East Indian Immigration to British Columbia and the Pacific Coast States," *The American Economic Review,* I (March, 1911), 24-75.

10. Followers of Guru Nanak (1469-1538), the Sikhs are generally domiciled in the Punjab. Fiercely monotheistic, they deny ritual, vestments, fanes, etc. Considered a militant sect, they recognize no distinction of caste. Center of worship is the sacred text, the *Granth Sahib.* Sikhs are identified by unshorn hair; wear short drawers and an iron bracelet; carry with them a comb and a steel dagger or sword. They considered themselves the community of the pure, the *Khalsa* and worship in temples called *gurdwaras.* They are noted for their charity and conscientious conformance to the ethical precepts of their religion. Sikhism is not to be considered a sect of Hinduism.

11. Khushwant Singh, *A History of the Sikhs* (Princeton: Princeton University Press, II, 175-76, and his *Ghadar 1915: India's First Armed Revolution* (New Delhi: R & K Publishing House, 1966) pp. 15-17.

12. There are a variety of accounts of the organization of the Hindu Association of the Pacific Coast citing different dates and different locations. For a further discussion of this, see Emily C. Brown, *Har Dayal: Hindu Revolutionist and Rationalist* (Tucson: University of Arizona Press, 1975), p. 138.

13. A file of *Ghadr* (in Gurmukhi) may be found at the New York Public Library. English translations are available in the Working Papers of the U.S. Attorney, California, Northern District, Neutrality Cases, 1913-1920: *U.S. v. Bopp, Ram Chandra et al.,* National Archives, Record Group 118.

14. *Lahore Conspiracy Case No. 1,* Judgement, September 13, 1915, Part III A (3), National Archives of India.

15. Brown, *op. cit.,* p. 155.

16. Har Dayal was never formally deported. Forfeiting bail, he left the country. Charges were subsequently dropped and the bail money returned.

17. U.S. Congress, House, Committee on Immigration, *Hearing, Restriction of Immigration of Hindu Laborers,* 63rd Congress, 2nd Session, 1914, Part I.

18. There is a great deal of material on the *Komagata Maru* incident. The best source on the India side is Gurdit Singh's own account: *Voyage of Komagatmaru or India's Slavery Abroad* (Calcutta: Gurdit Singh, n.d.). For the Canadian side, see Eric W. Morse, ''Some Aspects of the *Komagata Maru* Affair,'' *Report,* Canadian Historical Association (1936), pp. 100-108. An eye witness account of the resistance appeared in the Vancouver *Sun,* July 20, 1914. The article also included a reasonably objective summary of the whole affair.

19. *Ghadr,* August 4, 1914, *loc. cit.*

20. *Ghadr,* August 11, 1914, *loc. cit.*

21. Sir Michael Francis O'Dwyer, *India as I Knew It, 1885-1925* (London: Constable & Company. Ltd., 1925), p. 196.

22. Mention has already been made of Khushwant Singh's account of the Ghadr movement. The most complete account of the revolutionary activities is contained in Balshastri Hardas's *Armed Struggle for Freedom: Ninety Years War of Independence, 1857 to Subhash,* trans. S.S. Apte (Poona: Kal Prakashnan, 1958). The British side is told in the *Report of Committee Appointed to Investigate Revolutionary Conspiracies in India,* Cd 9190 (London: H. M. Stationery Office, 1918). This is more commonly known as the *Sedition Committee Report.*

23. American-Made Hindu Revolts,'' *The Literary Digest,* LI (July 10, 1915), 56.

24. Record of Trial in the District Court of the United States for the Southern Division of the Northern District of California, First Division. Before: Hon. William C. Van Fleet, Judge. *United States of America v. Franz Bopp et al. Defendants,* 75 vols. The full record is available at the India Office Library, London, and a microfilm copy is available at the University of California Library, Berkeley.

25. Brown, *op. cit.,* p. 202.

The Gadar Syndrome:
Ethnic Anger and Nationalist Pride

by

Mark Juergensmeyer*

In the first decades of this century, California provided the scene for one of the most bizarre and memorable incidents undertaken by any ethnic community in the United States: the attempt by a group of India's expatriate nationals to create a revolutionary army, invade India by sea, and liberate her from the clutches of British rule. A quixotic hope, and a tragic mission, as it turned out.

The Punjabis who organized it called their movement *Gadar* (alternately spelled Ghadar, or Ghadr). The name means "mutiny" or "revolt," and their mounting publicity actually led to such an attempt in 1915. Five boats, loaded with weapons and propaganda, set sail from various ports in California, financed by the German war effort. Alas, most were soon intercepted by the British. Those that landed were met by British authorities, and many leaders were hanged. Others were put on trial by the American government and many of them were deported.[1]

Curiously, the members of the movement were more militant than most of their nationalist compatriots back in India at that time. Theirs was an independent movement, existing almost solely in America, and its ties to India were remarkably weak. The poignancy of their endeavor is highlighted by their isolation: a stalwart band of rebels who maintained a lonely mutiny against British India, half a world away.

Then why did they do it? The answers to that question have ramifications beyond the Gadar incident, for as peculiar as Gadar may seem, it fits into a pattern of militant nationalism within expatriate communities that includes Irish nationalists, Chinese and Korean revolutionaries, and in our own time, Iranian militants. Within the Gadar case, then, is a syndrome of ethnic anger and nationalist pride, and the link between them begs to be understood.

Our explorations lead us in both directions from the Pacific: the American context and the Indian one. The Punjab context helps us under-stand why the immigrants came to America in the first place: the economic, social and political turmoil early in this century. The American context provides a hypothesis to explain how the frustrations of the new immigrant community were experienced as a double jeopardy, and turned into Gadar militancy. The hostility toward the prejudice of North American whites had identified itself with the nationalist struggle against the oppression in India. In America, the new immigrant community was trying to maintain its self-understanding as an Indian and a Sikh community, and developing its new identity as an ethnic working class, all in a climate of fear and suspicion. The struggle against the oppression in America and in India became fused into one struggle: Gadar.

The Gadar identity, then, was a compound of the nationalism and communalism which they brought from India, and the class consciousness and ethnic identity which they discovered in America. The former was a response to unjust British policies and tensions among Hindus, Muslims, and Sikhs in the Punjab, and the latter a response to economic and racial oppression in America. These elements comprised the mixed motives of the Gadar movement; they were reflected in the tensions within the organization, and echoed even in the composition of its membership.

The Mixed Constituency of the Movement

The Indians who came to the west coast of Canada and the United States around the turn of the century were mostly Punjabis, illiterate farmers and laborers, students and priests. The Gadar movement was an amalgam of these; and their social concerns were as varied as their occupations.

The movement included political refugees who found North America a congenial place to speak out against colonial rule. Har Dayal, the most visible and outspoken Gadar leader, came to the

United States as a visiting scholar; but he also came because of the greater political freedom which he perceived America to offer.[2] Ram Chandra, editor of the Gadar newspaper, and Barkatullah, an important strategist and liaison, were also involved in nationalist movements before they came to America. The Gadar movement could not have existed without their intellectual and political leadership, but their role should not be exaggerated. Har Dayal, for all his brilliance and charismatic authority, was an erratic leader, who left the movement and the United States in 1914, before the most critical years of the movement's history.

Immigrant laborers, farmers, and students provided the bulk of the movement's support. Baba Sohan Singh Bhakna, who is considered by some to be the founder of the Gadar movement, had been a laborer in a lumber mill in Oregon.[3] Jawala Singh, a potato farmer near Stockton, California, helped finance the movement; and Bhagwan Singh, who took over the Gadar party after the divisions within the party in 1917, was closely linked with the immigrant workers community as a *gyani* (priest). Kartar Singh Sarabha, the young martyred leader of the cadres who returned to foment an uprising in the Punjab in 1914-15, had come to the United States to be a student at the University of California, Berkeley.[4]

One would think that the immigrant workers and students had put India behind them. Even though their ties to their homeland may have been strong, one would have expected them to be emotionally detached from colonial oppression, and interested only in their own personal economic and scholarly achievements. Thus, the intense involvement of students and workers in the movement — their commitment unto death for a nationalist cause — can only be explained by the infusion of other, more personal, concerns.

Many of these personal concerns were linked with a universal problem of those in immigrant communities: that of being a stranger in a strange land. In the case of the immigrant Punjabis early in this century, that sense of strangeness was compounded by the experience of economic hardship and racial oppression. This may explain some of the Gadar intensity — the desire to turn the tables, and "drive the foreigners out of India,"[5] even as they in North America were the foreigners being driven out by the whites.

Formative Stages in Gadar History

In reviewing the development of the Gadar party, one notices a sort of rebound effect between acts of racial hostility against the immigrant Punjabis and new developments within the movement. There is also an interaction between events in the Punjab and the activities of the immigrant Punjabis. The two sets of relationships provide an incendiary crossfire.

The sequence of events was as follows: Oppressive British policies and communal tensions in the Punjab helped encourage migration to Canada and the United States, where those same issues were exacerbated by new racial tensions and oppressive policies of the Canadian and American governments. Thus, an irony of history emerges: the escape from colonialism and communalism leads to new forms of oppression and a sharper sense of ethnic identity and national pride.

The chart on the following page indicates events occurring in four contexts: the Punjab, the immigrant community, the anti-immigrant North Americans, and the Gadar movement. Some patterns emerge across these four columns which suggest that links may be hidden beneath them.

One such sequence of events may be traced from 1907 through 1913. In the Punjab context, a series of disturbances over British land rights legislation erupted in 1907.[6] The problem had been developing since 1900, when the Alienation of Land Act in India prohibited certain non-farming castes from owning agricultural lands.[7] The Act had the laudatory effect of preventing moneylenders from taking over farmland, but it irritated many middle-income non-agricultural Punjabis who had aspired to develop land. When new canal areas opened in the Punjab, government legislation prevented the settlers of these newly irrigated areas from full ownership. Added to these issues were the problems of nature — severe famine, and an epidemic of bubonic plague which allegedly took millions of lives.[8] The climate of hardship and government oppression resulted in a series of riots in the district towns of Punjab in the summer of 1907.

Events in Punjab	Activities of Immigrant Community	Response of North Americans	Developments in Gadar Movement
1900 - Alienation of Land Act			
	1906 - Immigration into British Columbia		
1907 - Riots in Punjab	1907-08 - Largest immigration: 5,000 in Canada 3,000 in U.S.	1907 - British Columbia Anti-Asiatic riots, Bellingham riots	
	1908 - Gurudwara, Trust	1908 - British Columbia stops immigration	
			1909 - Hindustan Association, British Columbia
	1910 - Last year of large immigration to U.S.	1910 - Oregon riots	1910 - Tarak Nath Das in Seattle 1911 - Arrival of Har Dayal
	1912 - Stockton Gurudwara		1912 - Hindustan Association, Oregon
		1913 - Alien Land Law	1913 - May: Hindi Association, Oregon Oct: Yuguntar Ashram, San Francisco Nov: *Ghadr* newspaper
		1914 - Wheatland, California Hop Riot	1914 - Komagata Maru Punjab invasion launched 1915 - Punjab invasion crushed
		1917 - Barred Zone Act	1917-18 - San Francisco trial
1919 - Jallianwallabagh Massacre			1919 - Reorganization of Gadar party
		1923 - Thind Case	1923 - New Gadar publications
		1924 - "Asian Exclusion Act"	1925 - Group of Gadarites join international communists.

Shifting to the immigrant context, we find that the years 1907 and 1908 were those of the largest number of immigrants to Canada and the United States.[9] The immigrants did not all come from the areas of the riots, and I have no hard evidence to indicate a direct relationship between the events in the Punjab and the immigration patterns. Nonetheless, the fact of unrest in the Punjab means that the emigrants, like everyone else, perceived the times to be in a state of flux, of political and social change, a signal for individuals to seek new opportunities and greater security.

Almost all of the immigrants were from Hoshiarpur, Jullundur and Ludhiana districts of central Punjab — an area dominated by peasant proprietors. The early 1900s was a time of varied mobility for them: many had migrated within Punjab to the new canal-irrigated colonies in southwestern Punjab. Eventually, in the United States, the Punjab immigrants also would be working in newly-irrigated farmlands in the San Joaquin Valley of California, which is geographically much like that area of the Punjab. But initially, in 1907 and 1908, the main destinations of the immigrants were the lumber camps of Oregon, Washington state, and British Columbia in Canada.[10] Many of the immigrants had come to North America via service in the British Army.[11] Most were Sikhs, and by the middle of 1908 they had begun building their own place of worship, a Gurdwara, in British Columbia, and establishing an investment company of their own, the Nanak Trust Co.[12]

On arrival the new immigrants from Punjab were met with hostility from some of the white residents of Canada and the United States. In most cases, the difficulties were in the competition for scarce jobs: the new immigrants were willing to do demanding work for less pay. In 1907 there were anti-Asian riots in British Columbia, in which Punjabis were targeted along with Chinese and Japanese; the same year, the Punjabis were the specific cause for riots in the lumber camps in Bellingham, Washington.[13] In 1908 and later, the riots had moved south to the state of Oregon, and in California, the Exclusion Movement against other Asians also included hostility against the Punjabis. And in 1908, British Columbia effectively ended all new Asian immigrations.[14]

These events in India, Canada and the United States were the immediate antecedents to the founding of the Hindustan Association in British Columbia in 1909, a precursor to the Gadar Movement, which advocated self-rule in India.[15] The Association did not directly respond to the labor problems and the racial prejudice encountered by the new immigrants, but clearly those economic and social tensions were in the background and gave fervor to its proclamations. During the busy years of 1907-1909, with so much traffic from India to North America, the events in the Punjab and the events abroad could not remain separate in the minds of the immigrant activists.

In 1910 through 1913, two other sequences of events appear. Restrictive legislation and racial disturbances had turned the focus of Punjabi emigration away from Canada and towards America: 1910 was the largest year of migration to the Unites States (until recent times). It was also a year of racial disturbances in both Oregon and California. The same year, Tarak Nath Das began agitating for Indian nationalism in Seattle, Washington,[16] and Har Dayal did the same in California after his arrival in February, 1911. Another group, calling itself the Hindustan Association, this one also a nationalist organization, was founded in Oregon in 1912.

By 1912, the immigrant community of Sikhs in California was sufficiently established to begin building its own Gurdwara, in Stockton.[17] The Punjabis (and other Asians) were also sufficiently established as landowners in the rich developing San Joaquin Valley farmland to threaten the resident American landowners.[18] In 1913, an Alien Land Law was passed, which limited land ownership for most Asians to three-year issues.[19] 1913 was also a critical year for the Gadar movement: in May, the Hindi Association was formed in Oregon by Har Dayal, Baba Sohan Singh Bhakna, and others. In October, Har Dayal had established the Yuguntar Ashram as a political headquarters of the movement in San Francisco; and in November, 1913, the newspaper *Ghadr* began publication.[20]

One of the most violent actions against the new Punjabi immigrants occurred in 1914, in Wheatland, California, where European and immigrant Asian laborers went on strike in the hop fields. The Asians, especially the Punjabis, received the brunt of the attacks from strikebreakers and anti-labor gangs. According to Professor Bruce LaBrack, members of the Punjabi immigrant community remember that event even today, and claim that it had much to do with the raising of their political consciousness. These feelings of outrage were transferred to hatred against the British, for they felt that if they controlled their own country, this sort of abuse would not have happened. The date of the riot is significant: in that same year, 1914, the Gadar party had its greatest expansion, and garnered widespread financial organizational support from the immigrant community.

The juxtaposition of events, of course, does not prove that there is a causative relationship. The political and demographic events in the Punjab may or may not have been the formative cause for the migrations; the life histories of many immigrants would have to be surveyed for that assertion to be proven.[21] Moreover, one cannot prove that the legislation and racial riots had a direct effect on the developments of the Gadar party, although there are some evidences of a correlation. According to G.B. Lal, an early member of the Ghadar movement interviewed by Professor Emily Brown, it was the task of the radical nationalist intellectuals, such as Kartar Singh Sarabha and Har Dayal, to make that link, and re-direct the interests of the immigrant community:

> We told them [the immigrant farmers] that it was no use to talk about the Asiatic Exclusion Act,[22] immigration, and citizenship. They had to strike at the British because they were responsible for the way Indians were being treated in America. There was some response. They made donations. They wanted to know what they could do. So we suggested that they start a newspaper and that they call it *Ghadr*.[23]

The sequences of events, while not conclusive, are tantalizing. In addition to the correlations we have mentioned above, later in Gadar's development there are even more correlative events: restrictive immigration laws and the German liaisons of World War I are coincident with such incidents as the Komagata Maru affair,[24] and the abortive Gadar uprising of 1915.[25] In the 1920s, the Thind Case in 1923 (in which an Indian immigrant attempted to escape restrictive clauses by arguing that Indians are Caucasian)[26] and the infamous "Asiatic Exclusion Act of 1924"[27] occur at the same time as the Gadar party's renewal and expansion into an international network.[28]

Although the sequential pattern of these events — in the Punjab, in the immigrant community, in the American response, and in the Gadar activity — is only suggestive, it does indicate that the experiences of the immigrant community in America were linked with Gadar events. The Gadar movement was undoubtedly genuine in expressing nationalist support for a free India; but at the same time it offered something more: a locus of identity and a channel of hostility for an angry and confused immigrant community.[28]

The Gadar Identity

The identity that Gadar provided was a compound of several elements, one of the most basic of which was economic. In the early days of the formation of the movement, from 1907 to 1912, when embryonic organizational meetings of the movement were held in British Columbia, Washington state, and Oregon, most of the immigrants were laborers in the lumber camps. There the issues of economic exploitation and class differentiation were prevalent.[30] Sohan Singh Bhakna, a key figure in the early pre-Gadar party meetings in Astoria, Oregon, who later returned to the Punjab to be a leader of the new communist party there, recalls that his socialist concerns had their origins in those early labor problems among the immigrant Punjabi lumber workers in Oregon.[31] It is clear that the Oregon meetings in 1912 and 1913 were concerned as much with labor issues as with nationalism.

When the center of Gadar activity shifted to California, however, the matter became more complicated. The movement which crystallized in San Francisco in 1913 was a mixture of intellectuals, political refugees, and farmers. The farmers were of several economic classes: some owned land (which they technically were supposed to abandon after American government legislation in 1913), others leased land, and others were landless laborers.[32] There is no indication that there was any tension among these different kinds of Indian participants in the movement; and there was no strong indication, in California, of the class identities and labor concerns that characterized the Oregon immigrant community.

Nonetheless, even in California the ingredients existed for class consciousness; and for some Gadarites that later blossomed into socialist ideology. The Gadar ideology before 1918 was almost exclusively nationalist, with a touch of utopian socialism brought to the movement by the visionary ideas of Har Dayal. His idiosyncratic vision, however, made very little impress upon the rest of the followers of the movement.[33] After the Russian revolution, experienced first-hand by some of the Gadarites returning to India between 1916 and 1919, Gadar ideology turned decisively to the left. In the 1920s, one wing of the old Gadar party was actively involved in international communism, and helped to formulate the communist party in the Punjab.[34]

The Marxism of some of the later Gadarites is a mark of the apparent secularity of the movement. Yet if one looks closely at the character of the immigrant community supporting Gadar, one finds a strikingly religious strand. On the movement's publications one finds the names "Ram, Allah and Nanak" on the masthead, an invitation of membership to all those who revere those three divine names. And the movement did, in fact, include members of the differing faiths: Har Dayal and Ram Chandra were both Hindus: Bhagwan Singh and Kartar Singh Sarabha, Sikhs; and Barkatullah, Muslim.

Yet the overwhelming numbers of supporters of the movement were Sikh, and their militant religious history also became a part of the Gadar identity. Among the immigrant farmers who supplied money and labor, Sikhs predominated, and provided the movement's mass base. After Har Dayal had left the United States for Europe in 1915, and Ram Chandra was shot during the 1918 San Francisco trial, the Sikhs under the leadership of Bhagwan Singh had the movement almost to themselves.[35]

Sikh institutions and organizations also played an important role in the movement. The first Indian nationalist organization in British Columbia was closely related to the Khalsa Diwan Society of the Sikh Gurdwara there, and the later Gadar movement had a symbiotic relationship to the Khalsa Diwan Society and the Sikh Gurdwara in Stockton — sometimes mutually supportive, sometimes competitive. After 1920, the wing of the movement in the San Joaquin Valley of California was, for all practical purposes, a Sikh organization. There were even some Sikhs who regarded members of the Gadar movement as *Sant Sapahis,* warriors for the faith.

This identification of Gadar with Sikhs does not mean, however, that the movement was ever overtly religious; the movement's ideology was always political, untainted with the language of faith. Yet, like much else in India, the religious and the social aspects were frequently intertwined, and neither element is without some trace of the other. Perhaps, then, it would be better to describe Gadar's religious character as a communal identity for many of the Sikhs who supported the movement and found in it the fulfillment of some of their cultural and social needs. Again, there was an American echo to a situation of stress in India: in Punjab, during the first decades of this century, the Sikh community was going through a period of self-definition, in response to the communalism of urban Hindus and Muslims.[36] Within the Gadar movement in America, that awareness of identity was fused with an immigrant community's own attempt to define and understand itself in a strange land.

Gadar as Ethnic Identity

Gadar was the expression of an immigrant community, and beneath its intense nationalism there is the awkward self-image of a group of people who were no longer in India, but not quite yet within North America. The syndrome was beginning to emerge: a native nationalism that they felt when they were within the boundaries of other countries, in part because of the strangeness of their new surroundings, and in part because of the inability of the new country to accept them.[37] These were some of the dynamics in the nationalism of Gandhi in South Africa a few years before, and they became part of the motivation of those who founded Gadar.

One may view the Gadar nationalism as a form of escape, or as an attempt at accommodation. In the hostile environment of North American prejudice, the Indian nationalism gave the immigrant community the illusion that they were a part of India, and therefore free from the racial problems of North America. At the same time, Gadar's nationalism provided the immigrant community with an ethnic identity, a sense of pride, which enabled them to stand up to the difficulties of their hostile North American environment.

Both views are apt, but initially it was the former interpretation — nationalism as a link between the immigrant community and its homeland — that characterized the founding spirit. By remaining nationalistically Indian through the Gadar movement, the founders distanced themselves from the pejorative image of being a part of a minority community in a foreign society. By keeping their Indian identities, they also kept alive the possibility that they might return to India. But as the immigrant community became more settled, and the Gadar movement became more integrated with the life of the community, the Gadar nationalism became fused with their identity as ethnic Indian-Americans. This appears to be the case especially after 1920. In the early 1920s, when the movement fragmented, one section of the Gadar movement became a platform for local politics and immigrant community organization.

There were hints of this role even earlier. The movement had helped to identify and train leaders and had given them a basis of support. Having had a certain concentration of money and influence, Gadar became an arena of power within the immigrant community. In 1915 through 1917, when it was torn apart by two rival factions, the issue was as much a struggle for dominance as it was a difference of ideology. The shocking death of Ram Chandra, and the succession of Gyani Bhagwan Singh to the mantle of Gadar leadership in 1918 was a dramatic indication of the importance attached to the internal power of the party.[39]

The movement continued as a source of ethnic identity and nationalist pride through the 1930s and formally came to a demise only at the time of India's independence. In the later years it was more and more an element of the immigrant community identity. When a U.S. citizen of Punjabi descent ran for the American House of Representatives in the 1950s, his tenuous link with the Gadar party became a serious campaign

issue, since Gadar had become linked with international communism.[40] During the McCarthy era of the 1950s, the entire Punjabi immigrant community in California feared the revenge of a paranoid America against them. Only recently has academic research into the immigrant community and Gadar been possible again, now that the red scare of the 1950s has subsided.[41] Once again the movement can only be discussed by the community, and has again become a symbol of its nationalist pride.

That symbol has recently taken shape in the form of a building. In 1975, the government of India constructed a handsome redwood library and meeting hall at 5 Wood Street, San Francisco, on the site of the original headquarters of the Gadar party. Most of the funds to construct the Ghadar Memorial Library came from Punjabis living in California. In addition to serving as a museum and library, the building is used as a meeting hall for the local community. Thus, the name of Gadar continues to be identified with the ethnic pride of the children and grandchildren of the original Gadar rebels.

The Gadar Syndrome

In brief, then, the "Gadar Syndrome" may be described as follows: A militant nationalist movement is created abroad by expatriates, for whom the movement is also an outlet for their economic and social frustrations, and a vehicle for their ethnic identities. It is the fusion and the mutual interaction of ethnic anger and nationalist pride.

Viewed as a general type, a syndrome, Gadar does not stand alone. There were other ethnic communities in the United States for whom ethnicity and nationalist pride came together in a revolutionary movement. The immigrant Irish laborers, for example, were waging their own struggle against the British at the time of the Gadar movement, and the members of the Irish community in California became Gadar's close allies. The Gadar party, in turn, printed tracts in favor of Irish independence.[42] After the death of Ram Chandra, members of the Irish independence movement befriended the family, and supported other members of the movement.[43]

Among other Asian communities one finds further instances of the Gadar syndrome.[44] The 1911 revolution led by Sun Yat Sen occurred during a time when the Chinese immigrants in the United States were the subjects of social prejudice and restrictive legislation, similar to that experienced by the Punjab immigrants, and the active support of the Sun Yat Sen revolution by immigrant Chinese was not altogether unlike the revolutionary activities of the Gadarites.[45] In 1910, Sun Yat Sen came to America to organize chapters of his revolutionary organization, the Tongmenghui, which in alliance with local organizations "emerged as a significant political force in Chinese communities in the U.S. and Canada."[46] Korean nationalist activities in the United States also paralleled those of the Gadar syndrome.[47]

Thus, even though the Gadar movement may hold a peculiar place in the history of India's struggle for independence, it is not an isolated incident in the pattern of ethnic communities in the United States. Viewed from the perspective of India, the Gadar revolutionaries' earnest but unsuccessful contribution to the task of independence is something of an enigma. But viewed from the perspective of North America, the activities of the Gadar rebels appear quite different. In the American context, the movement is, in part, the expression of an oppressed minority community. The anger and humiliation was reversed into pride — a nationalist pride — which sharpened into the militant potency of Gadar, and its futile revolution.

FOOTNOTES

*   Mark Juergensmeyer is an Associate Professor of Religious Studies at the Graduate Theological Union and the University of California, Berkeley, CA 94709.

1.   The movement underwent a revival in the 1920s, with cadres of Punjabis active in various Asian and European countries, in addition to San Francisco. There are relatively few scholarly accounts of the Gadar party written in the United States, but a number of works are available in India, including A.C. Bose, *Indian Revolutionaries Abroad* (Patna: Bharati Bhawan, 1971); G.S. Deol, *The Role of the Ghadar Party in the National Movement* (Delhi: Sterling Publishers, 1969); L.P. Mathur, *Indian Revolutionary Movement in the United States of America* (Delhi: S. Chand & Co., 1970); G.S. Sainsara, *et. al., Ghadar Party da Itihas* (in Punjabi) (Jullundur: Desh Bhagat Yaad Ghar Committee, 1961); Khushwant Singh and Satindra Singh, *Ghadar, 1915: India's First Armed Revolution* (Delhi: R & K Publishing House, 1966); and Harish K. Puri, *The Ghadar Party: A Study in Militant Nationalism* (Dept. of Political Science, Guru Nanak University, Amritsar, 1975). An overview of the literature is given in Mark Juergensmeyer, "The International Heritage of the Ghadar Party: A Survey of the Sources," in the American journal, *Sikh Sansar* vol. 2, no. 1, March 1973, a revised version of which appears in N.G. Barrier and Harban Singh, eds., *Punjab Past and Present: Essays in Honor of Dr. Ganda Singh* (Patiala: Punjabi University Press, 1976). An earlier form of this paper was presented at the 1976 Sikh Studies Conference at Berkeley and published in its proceedings.

2.   See Emily Brown, *Har Dayal: Hindu Revolutionary and Rationalist* (Tucson: The University of Arizona Press, 1975).

3.   See Sohan Singh Josh, *Baba Sohan Singh Bhakna: Life of the Founder of the Ghadar Party* (New Delhi: People's Publishing House, 1970).

4.   A fictional account of Kartar Singh's life has received popular acclaim in the Punjab, *Ik Mian, Do Talwaran* ("One Scabbard, Two Swords") by Nanak Singh (Delhi: Navayug Publishers, 1963). See also Mark Juergensmeyer, "India's Berkeley Radical," in the Sunday edition of *Times of India,* March 6, 1977.

5.   The cry, *ferenghi maro* ("destroy the foreigner") frequently appeared in Gadar literature.

6.   See Sri Ram Sharma, *Punjab in Ferment in the Beginning of the Twentieth Century* (Patiala: Punjabi University Department of Punjab Historical Studies, 1966); and N.G. Barrier, "Punjab Politics and the Disturbances of 1907" (Ph.D. dissertation, Duke University, 1966).

7.   The Alienation of Land Act allowed the traditional agricultural castes, such as Jats, to retain rights to the land, while disallowing such rights to urban Khatri, Arora and other merchant castes. Lower castes and Untouchables were also excluded, since it was feared that they would be used as a front for upper castes to purchase land. The adverse effect of the Act was to stabilize caste mobility, and to strengthen the divisions of society along caste lines. See N.G. Barrier, *The Punjab Alienation of Land Bill 1900* (Durham: Duke University South Asia Series, 1965).

8.   The economic and social effects of these disasters, and the continuing problem of moneylenders, are described in Sir Malcolm Darling, *The Punjab Peasant in Prosperity and Debt* (London: Oxford University Press, 1925). A useful summary of the statistics from government reports on the difficult economic conditions in the Punjab around the turn of the century may be found in chapter 10, "Rural Indebtedness and Peasant Agitation; of Kushwant Singh's *History of the Sikhs*, Vol. II (Princeton: Princeton University Press, 1966).

9. The official statistics of the Canadian government show that over 5,000 immigrants from India entered Canada between 1905 and 1913, almost all of them in the years 1907 and 1908 (2,124 and 2,623, respectively) (cited in R.K. Das, *Hindustani Workers on the Pacific Coast,* Berlin, 1923). Official records in the United States indicate a similar number, between 1900 and 1917; the largest number of entries in the United States was around 1910. However, the real number of immigrants was probably quite a bit greater, allowing for illegal entries. One scholar has simply doubled the official figures for her own working estimate (Joan M. Jensen, "Federal Policy in the Shaping of Indian Occupations in the United States, 1900 - 1917," paper delivered at the Western Conference of the Association for Asian Studies, 1974, Tempe, Arizona).

10. Some of the immigrants who worked in the British Columbia lumber mills had had previous acquaintance with the lumber industry in India, in their home area of Hoshiarpur, a Punjab district with abundant forest lands.

11. Estimates are as high as 75% of the immigrant males having served in the army. Conditions of economic and social unrest in the Punjab which encouraged immigration also encouraged participation in the army, so it is not surprising that a high number of persons would seek both options of opportunity in sequence.

12. These indications of the immigrants' initial prosperity come from old interviews, cited in Harish Puri, "The Ghadar Party: A Study in Militant Nationalism" (Ph.D. dissertation in Political Science, Guru Nanak Dev University, Amritsar, 1975), p. 39.

13. These and other incidents are summarized in R.K. Das, *op. cit.,* and A.C. Bose, *Indian Revolutionaries Abroad* (Patna: Bharati Bhawan, 1971).

14. Harish Puri has raised an interesting argument regarding the motivation for Canadian exclusion against the Punjabis. According to Puri (*op. cit.,* pp. 50-51), the Punjabis were excluded, among other reasons, because their residency in Canada would be used for anti-British purposes. Puri marshals two pieces of evidence indicating this fear among the British: a statement by Colonel Swayne, seriously discussed by the British India office, which claimed that "dissatisfaction at unfair treatment of Indians in Vancouver is certain to be exploited for the purpose of agitation in India;" and the fact that the Indians were excluded more harshly than Japanese and Chinese. Puri may be correct; but the fact of racial and economic prejudice against the immigrant community made the exclusionary restrictions possible.

15. A series of newspapers began to be published in British Columbia about this time, 1907-1909, with names such as *Free Hindustan, Aryan,* and *Swadesh Sewak;* microfilmed copies of some of the issues are on file at the University of British Columbia, Vancouver. The dominant theme of the newspapers is nationalist and anti-British, but some articles reflect the local concerns of the immigrant community, especially regarding immigration laws and economic problems.

16. Tarak Nath Das came to the United States in 1906 as a student at the University of California, Berkeley, but soon went to Canada to agitate for nationalist causes among the immigrant community in British Columbia before returning to the United States via Washington and Oregon, where he continued to be involved in nationalist organization. Tarak Nath Das survived the difficulties that the Gadar party later encountered, and later in his life became a distinguished professor of international relations at Columbia University, New York.

17. There is still a Gurdwara in Stockton called a "Sikh temple." Most of the Punjabi immigrants have shifted further north in the San Joaquin Valley of California, where they have recently erected a handsome new Gurdwara near the city of Marysville.

18. One of the immigrant farmers, Jawala Singh, had become so wealthy through the production of potatoes that he was called the "potato king." The San Joaquin Valley of California is remarkably similar in climate and demography to the irrigated areas of the Punjab; so the immigrant Punjabis had a familiarity with farming techniques which gave them an advantage over the American settlers of the newly irrigated areas of the San Joaquin Valley. The Punjabis' use of skillful techniques, their ability to work hard and save their earnings, are described in Bruce La Brack, "Occupational Specialization of California Sikhs: The Interplay of Culture and Economics," a paper presented at the Fifth Punjab Studies Conference, Berkeley, California, March 21-23, 1975.

19. The prohibition against owning land not only dampened the economic development of many of the immigrant Punjabis, it also limited their outlets for investment of their savings. Some of the money used to support the Gadar party came from immigrant farmers who might otherwise have used it to purchase land, or invest in equipment.

20. It is these events that begin most accounts of the Gadar "Party," which restrict their time span to the years of 1913 through 1917. If one regards Gadar as a movement, in a more general way, the history would begin in 1907, when the first nationalist meetings occurred, and continue at least into the 1930s.

21. Quite a few life histories of Gadar members exist, many of them collected for the composite history written by Gurcharan Singh Sainsra, *op. cit.,* and which are now on file in the Desh Bhagat Yaad Ghar in Jullundur City, Punjab. These are not a representative sampling, but they do indicate that the immigrants were motivated by the problems at home as well as the opportunities abroad.

22. There is no Act formally entitled "Asiatic Exclusion Act." The U.S. Immigration and Naturalization Act of 1924 is often called the Oriental (or Asiatic) Exclusion Act; but G.B. Lal is probably referring to the Alien Land Law of 1913, which restricted Asian immigrants' rights to own land.

23. Emily Brown, *Har Dayal: Hindu Revolutionary and Rationalist* (Tucson: University of Arizona Press, 1975), p. 141. *Ghadar,* and other publications of the Gadar movement which are extant or have been translated by the U.S. government and introduced as evidence during the trial of *U.S.A. vs Franz Bopp* (now in the U.S. archives in San Bruno, California), are almost exclusively concerned with nationalist and anti-British issues. The link between the concerns of the immigrant community and the nationalism of the Gadar movement is to be found in the life histories of the participants (e.g., Sohan Singh Bhakna, *op. cit.,* the unpublished autobiographical account of the Gadar movement by B. Chenchiah on file in the Desh Bhagat Yaad Ghadr, Prithvi Singh Azad's *Kranti Path Ka Pathik,* and Nand Singh Sihra's article in *Modern Review,* August 1913, "Indians in Canada: A Pitiable Account of Their Hardships by One Who Comes from the Place and Knows Them").

24. The ship, Komagata Maru, was chartered by a group of Punjab immigrants in an attempt to circumvent a devious Canadian regulation which denied entry to any immigrant who did not arrive on a vessel sailing directly from the immigrant's homeland; at the time, no such ship sailed from India. The Komagata Maru was not allowed to land anyway. This incident was directly responsible for new converts to the Gadar cause, and greatly encouraged the movement. Two books chronicle the tale: Sohan Singh Josh, *The Tragedy of the Komagata Maru* (New Delhi: People's Publishing House, 1975), and Ted Ferguson, *A White Man's Country: An Exercise in Canadian Prejudice* (Toronto: Doubleday Canada Ltd., 1975).

25. The attempted Gadar uprising in 1915 benefitted by World War I in two ways: it hoped that the British army would be so distracted by the war that they would not be able to control the anticipated uprising; and, more directly, the Gadarites received support from the British enemies, the Germans, in the form of money, advice, and some arms.

26. "United States vs. Bhagat Singh Thind, Feb. 19, 1923," *Supreme Court Reporter* vol. 43, no. 10.

27. Officially titled "The Immigration and Naturalization Act of 1924," the so-called "Asiatic Exclusion Act" applied to Chinese and Japanese, as well as South Asians, and was not fully repealed until the U.S. Immigration and Nationality Act of 1965.

28. There was also an active attempt to link the Gadar cause with America's tradition of independence; pictures of Washington and Lincoln appeared in the Gadar papers, and in the 1920s a new Gadar newspaper was entitled *The United States of India.*

29. The immigrant context might be the cause of the disintegration of the Gadar movement, as well as the rise of it. As the community was more accepted into society, parochial identities emerged. Tensions between Hindu/Sikh, urban/rural elements within the Gadar party were part of the reason for the movement's decline after 1917. Later, other fissures arose between the Jats and non-Jats, and between doaba Punjabis and those from Ludhiana, Ferozepur, and Amritsar.

30. Harish Puri, *op. cit.*

31. See Sohan Singh Bhakna's autobiography, *Jeewan Sangram* (Jullundur: Yuvak Kender Prakashan, 1967).

32. Many of the laborers in the fields of California were of higher castes, and would not have engaged in such occupations in India. Only one Gadar activist, Mangoo Ram, was from a Scheduled Caste; he later became the leader of the Ad Dharm movement on his return to India. See Appendix A, "The Early Life of Mangoo Ram," in my *Religion as Social Vision: The Movement Against Untouchability in 20th Century Punjab* (Berkeley: University of California Press, 1982).

33. G.B. Lal, a colleague of Har Dayal, said that "most of the members of the Party did not understand Har Dayal's finer teachings, only the nationalism" (interview with G.B. Lal, April 1973).

34. The relationship of former Gadarites to the Punjab Communist Party is described in Tilak Raj Chadha's "Punjab's Red and White Communists: Scramble for Funds from America," *Thought,* June 14, 1952. The international connections are described by Gail Omvedt in "Armed Struggle in India: The Ghadar Party," *Frontier,* November 9, 1974 and November 16, 1974.

35. It is not fair to describe the factional disputes within the Gadar organization as Hindu versus Sikh; nonetheless, the assassination of Ram Chandra by a Sikh removed the last Hindu intellectual of significance from the movement's leadership.

36. The Singh Sabha and the Gurudwara Reform Movement are evidences of this identity consciousness.

37. There were, no doubt, many kind and gracious white Americans who did accept the new Punjabi immigrants with generosity. Unfortunately, there were a sufficient number of others to create a climate of uneasiness about the presence of the new immigrants. The popular press wrote about the "turbaned tide" from India; and at the very extreme was hate-literature, such as the tract, *The White Man,* which contained articles such as "The Hindu: The Filth of Asia." Even in recent years, the immigrant Punjabis in California are sometimes called "ragheads."

38. It was in South Africa, in 1893-1915, that Gandhi's nationalism first developed. See M.K. Gandhi, *Satyagraha in South Africa,* translated by V.G. Desai (Ahmedabad: Navajivan Trust, first published in 1928).

39. The motivation for the murder of Ram Chandra has never been settled, but the event occurred in the context of the U.S. government trial against Gadar for its complicity with the Germans *(U.S. vs. Franz Bopp, et.al.),* which exacerbated the existing factional tensions within the movement. See the interview with Mrs. Chandra on file in the Gadar collection of the South Asia Library Service, University of California, Berkeley, and also Bhagwan Singh's *Brief Sketch of Life Lived,* issued by the department of public relations, Government of Punjab, 1948.

40. Dilip Singh Saund won the election, and became the first person of Asian ancestry to sit in the U.S. House of Representatives. See D.S. Saund, *Congressman from India* (New York: E.P. Dutton & Co., 1960).

41. Among the new researchers are Jane Singh of the University of California, Berkeley; Karen Leonard of the University of California, Irvine; and Bruce LaBrack of the University of the Pacific, Stockton. LaBrack has compiled an extensive bibliography on the immigrant community, "The East Indian Experience in America," which is serialized in the journal *Sikh Sansar* (Redwood City, California, 1976-77 issues). The most comprehensive early research on the community was undertaken by Professor Harold Jacoby, also of the University of the Pacific.

42. One such pamphlet was *Hindustan atte Ireland,* a translation of a speech by the President of the Irish Republic.

43. Interview with Mrs. Ram Chandra, Gadar Collection, South Asia Library Service (University of California, Berkeley, 1973).

44. One would suspect this to be the case, since the patterns of Indian immigration were roughly similar to those of other Asian communites; see Sucheng Chan, "Overseas Sikhs in the Context of Asian Migrations," in Mark Juergensmeyer and N.G. Barrier, eds., *Sikh Studies: Working Papers of the 1976 Summer Conference* (Berkeley Religious Series of America, 1978).

45. A summary of the legislation to exclude Chinese is given in Thomas W. Chinn, ed., *A History of the Chinese in California: A Syllabus* (San Francisco: Chinese Historical Society of America, 1969), pp. 23-30.

46. H. Mark Lai, "China Politics and the U.S. Chinese Communities," *Counterpoint: Perspectives on Asian America,* ed. by Emma Gee (Los Angeles: 1976), p. 154.

47. See Kingsley K. Lyu, "Korean Nationalist Activities in Hawaii and America, 1901-1945," in Gee, *op. cit.*

Immigration Law and the Revitalization Process:
The Case of the California Sikhs[1]

by

Bruce La Brack*

In 1956, Dr. Harold Jacoby reviewed the history and social position of Indian and Pakistani immigrants in America in a short research report titled, *A Half-Century Appraisal of East Indians in the United States.*[2] At that time there were less than 3,000 persons of South Asian origin in the U.S. and of that number only half were permanent residents. I briefly considered writing an article titled, *A Three Quarter Century Appraisal of East Indians in the United States,* but desisted, because I was overwhelmed with the enormity of the task which would be necessary to deliver such an update. Not only has the South Asian component grown some 1200% (the iterim census of 1980 reporting 361,544 persons under category of 'Asian Indian')[3] but the ethnic, racial, social, economic, occupational, religious, and educational diversity of the contemporary South Asian segment is enormous. It will never again be possible to easily categorize and summarize the cultural and social characteristics of America's Asian Indian population. Nevertheless, regardless of the current complexity of their American societies, all South Asian communities are to some extent a product of immigration and subject to the vicissitude of what has been at times a particularly arbitrary legal system. Although America is truly a "nation of immigrants," the flow of certain immigrant populations has not been a steady current, but rather one marked by periodic vacillation, reversal, exclusion, and discrimination. While it would be difficult and perhaps even egregious to say that South Asians have suffered more under these fluctuating policies than any other Asian groups, one thing is certain: for over a quarter of a century their legal rights were dictated by immigration policy and it would be difficult to find any important area of their lives which was not touched upon as a result of changes in immigration laws. Mar-

riage, family, ownership of land, voting rights, political freedom, free-entry and exit of the country, and citizenship where all affected by political decisions made on racial and social grounds. This paper will review some of these negative effects, most of which occurred in the pre-1947 period, but the major thrust will be to outline how changes in recent immigration laws, particularly since 1965 have led to not only a dramatically increased population growth, but also to community revitalization.

What immigration laws take away they can, under certain circumstances, restore. However, the simple physical addition of people to a country does not automatically insure a resurgence of ethnic identity, religious revitalization, or social life. Therefore, some of the major characteristics of this community revival will be discussed using a Sikh community in the Northern Sacramento Valley of California as a case study and point of comparison.

Although the time between 1906 (the first year of large-scale immigration of Asian Indians to the U.S.), and the reopening of immigration from India in 1947, is a period of great interest to political scientists and historians, from a sociological perspective it can be characterized as a short burst of immigration (1904-1917) followed by a long decline, physical and cultural. The summary of immigration history is simple to detail. It began with an unexpected (and unwanted) increase in immigration to North America by natives of what was the South Asian portion of the British Empire in 1904. Alarm over this new development led rather directly to tri-lateral talks between the British, Indian and Canadian governments which resulted in ending Indian immigration to Canada in 1909.[4] In the U.S. anti-Oriental agitation was in evidence early in 1907 and continued well into World War II, but the exclusionary forces achieved their aim legally in 1917 with the passage of what was popularly known as the "Barred Zone" provision.[5] Although primarily designed to restrict immigration from southern and eastern Europe, the net effect was to exclude from the U.S. unskilled laborers (who had formed the bulk of the initial East Indian immigration) from all of Asia except Japan. The cessation of immigration was followed in 1923 with the denial and even recension of citizenship after Justice Sutherland rendered a negative opinion in the Thind case, judging that "Hindus" were not "white persons." In addition to these liabilities, some states, California among them, passed Alien Land Laws and similar legislation to impede or stop acquisition, ownership, and even leasing of land or commercial property by "aliens."

The result of these immigration restrictions and other forces (World War I, the Great Depression, World War II) the Asian Indian population, which never exceeded 10,000 at its height, began a decline in the 1920's which continued up to the end of World War II, offset only slightly by an illegal immigration in the 20's and 30's of perhaps 3,000 or more men.[6] The all-male nature of the immigration (sex ratio was probably 75:1 at its *most* favorable)[7] and the migratory or hired-hand occupational level of the majority of the early immigrants insured a life-style quite different from either that they would have chosen in their home country or that of the dominant American society which surrounded them. The natural decline of the population through mortality was compounded as men who were not married could not bring brides from India and married men could not bring their wives or children to America. Non-endogamic marriage, although practiced widely, was a pragmatic option to the single life, not a preferred alternative, and it appears that the unions were far more fragile than traditional Indian marriages in which both partners were from the same cultural and religious background. By 1950 the total U.S. Asian Indian population was a minuscule, and still declining, 1500 or so persons.

What had begun as an immigration of male sojourners in search of fortune, turned out to be in some ways a legal entrapment. Once here and established, the Asian Indian man found himself after 1917 unable either to bring his family to the U.S. nor could he himself leave

the country because it was likely he would not be readmitted. The changes in the immigration laws between 1917 and 1924 not only restricted but resulted in a kind of encapsulation. Certain federal pressures towards occupational channeling when coupled with traditional orientations towards farming, almost assured a certain degree of social isolation.[8] Adding the natural tendency of the various Asian Indian socio-religious groups to form their own organizations and maintain their customs to whatever extent circumstances permit, the degree of social integration with the larger American society was minimal, with a few notable exceptions.

Finally, the high percentage of exogamous marriages to Catholic women of Spanish-backgrounds tended to create a half-way generation of half-Asian Indian-half-Mexican children.[9] As this second generation grew up its understanding and appreciation of their fathers' religion and society was often rather sketchy and incomplete. The late 1940's and 1950's was the midpoint in the shift from all-male or Asian Indian-Mexican family to the more traditional all-Asian Indian family which became the norm in the resurgence of the Asian Indian population which began in the late 1960's and continues to the present. Due to the impossibility of maintaining an Indian social structure in the American context and the fact that many Asian Indians took a very liberal view of religious affiliation, the children of Asian Indian-Mexican unions were raised in a Catholic, Spanish/Mexican social milieu, the social beliefs and religious practices of the father remaining largely a personal matter. The few references by social scientists to the Hindus, Muslims and Sikhs of California in the 50's and even 60's, speak of terms of assimilation, amalgamation, and integration of the Asian Indian segments, although writers varied in their interpretation of how 'assimilable' the Asian groups would be.

The continuation of the decline into the early 1950's is interesting because it illustrates two points. First, regardless of the fact that in 1946 the Luce-Celler Bill[10] removed all former immigration liabilities and granted a "Quota" of 100 persons a year from India, there was no rush for applications. Second, in the enthusiasm of the moment for the newly Independent India, many men returned to India, some never to return to the U.S. while others returned only years later. The opening turned out in retrospect to be more symbolic than real; between 1948 and 1965 less than 5,200 people from the subcontinent were admitted, or an average of 300 per year.

The decline, from a cultural standpoint, was even more severe. Economic and educational profiles of those Asian Indians remaining in the late 1940's show that most had remained farm laborers, farmers, or farm foremen/managers (65%), the majority of these agriculturally-oriented populations residing in California where sixty percent of all Asian Indians in the U.S. lived according to the 1940 census.[11] Fewer than four percent had become professionals, or more accurately, had remained in professional capacities. A number of Asian Indians who immigrated to the U.S., particularly those from urban areas, had some professional or technical training, but were unable to find comparable work here and were forced to take up whatever manual labor was available. In California the "factories in the fields" provided ample opportunity, particularly in the early years when Chinese and Japanese labor was becoming unavailable and politically unacceptable.[12] Taking all labor classifications, the Asian Indian population by 1940 was eighty-five percent blue-collar.

It was also rapidly becoming geriatric as sixty-six percent were over forty years of age, thirty-two percent over fifty, and nine percent over sixty. Median school years of education completed was by far the lowest at 3.7, and of those over twenty-five years of age more than a third had no formal education whatsoever. Even number of children per family for those who had married while here (approximately 50% did so) was rather small, overall averaging 2.4 children per family, moreover the majority of these marriages were with Spanish or Mexican-American women.[13] The statistical picture which emerges is of a relatively-isolated, rural-based, agriculturally-oriented, aging, and uneducated group who had generally married late and with non-Asian Indian partners. Thus, the overall effects the restrictive legislation begun in 1917 had taken its toll by the late 1940's and there were few 'communities' of Asian Indians left that would qualify even under the most liberal inter-

pretation of the term. Most of those which did survive were in California and did so precisely because of their small numbers, rural base, and unobtrusive deportment. Nevertheless, the reopening once again made legal immigration of South Asians possible and this fact precipitated a number of events which foreshadow some of the later cultural developments in California Sikh communities. First, men who had been separated from their wives and families could be reunited, some after as much as thirty years. Few separations were that extreme, but ten to fifteen years were not uncommon. This shows the strength of the marriage bond and familial commitments even in the face of long separations and legal restrictions which should have been permanent. In other cases, Asian Indian men who had been married when they came to America later married Mexican women. Generally when it became apparent that their stay might be indefinite with no possibility of reunion with their original family. When India became free they divorced the Spanish wives and returned to India for their first bride. Technically bigamy, such cases were never retrospectively prosecuted as the first marriage was never recorded in the U.S. Additionally, a number of older men who had been widowed while in the U.S. or who had never been married, returned home for Indian brides, most of these marriages being arranged in the traditional manner. In all cases this demonstrates a strong preference for endogamous marriage, regardless of intervening or temporary circumstances.

Before looking specifically at the results of this reopening of immigration on California Sikh communities, the larger immigration picture should be sketched out and brought up to date. The years between 1948 and 1965 were rather static, immigration averaging around 250-300 a year,[14] including both 'quota' and non-quota categories. As abruptly as the 1917 Immigration Act halted the flow of immigrants from India, the October 3rd Immigration and Nationality Act of 1965 restored a much freer exchange.[15] Specifically it abolished the "Quota" system and replaced a specific numerical limit for individual countries with a system in which Eastern and Western Hemispheres had annual quota limits, 170,000 being the limit for the Eastern Hemisphere — including all of the South Asian continent. This category covered both immigrants who came as 'green card' or resident visa holders and those who had their status changed to that of permanent resident. The only restrictions under the numerical limitation was a limit of 20,000 from any one country. In effect, the old quota of 100 was raised 2000%. In addition there was an additional category which was termed "immigrants exempt from numerical limitations." This was intended as an open immigration category to be restricted to 'immediate family,' defined as parents, spouses, or children.

The immediate effect of this relaxation of immigration laws on the entire Asian component of U.S. society was, and continues to be, dramatic. It was several years before the nondiscriminatory 1965 act was to have a full impact, but as Daniels noted, "by the years 1969, 1970 1971. . . immigrants from Asia comprised between 15 and 20 percent of all immigrants, the highest percentage in U.S. history."[16] He also noted that more than half of them live in two states, California and Hawaii. Table I gives some indication of the magnitude of the Asian Indian immigration.

TABLE 1

EFFECT OF OCTOBER 3RD, 1965 ACT ON ASIAN INDIAN POPULATION GROWTH[18] IN THE UNITED STATES TO 1975

	Period	Immigrants Admitted
1947	1941-1950	1,761
Quota	1951-1960	1,973
1965	1961-1965	2,602
	1966	2,458
	1967	4,642
	1968	4,682
	1969	5,963
Act of	1970	10,114
October 3rd		
	1971	14,310
	1972	16,926
	1973	13,124
	1974	12,779
	1975	15,773

The overall changes have, of course, not been limited to Asian Indians as all other Asian and Pacific groups previously under some quota were also affected by the new limits. Substantial

Korean, Vietnamese, and other minority groups had come in substantial numbers by the mid-1970's and continue to do so. The entire U.S. demographic pattern had been altered. Even limiting consideration to Asian Indians, excluding Pakistanis who are listed separately (and ignoring the 1972 Bangladesh secession), the numerical increase of immigrants has gone from 582 in 1965 to 14,733 in 1975, a percentage increase of +2,610.1 in one decade.[17] It is the largest jump for any one national category of immigrant; however, it must be remembered that the base number was very small, so the absolute increase is not that great, perhaps 100,000 Asian Indians resided in the U.S. as of 1975,[18] and possibly 360,000 in 1980.

More important than sheer volume, are the social and occupational profiles of the new immigrants. Such data shows them to be a largely well-educated, relatively affluent group from the middle and upper-middle classes of urban Indian society. Many are professionals with a high percentage of educators, physicians, lawyers, accountants, engineers, and research scientists. Obviously they differ in nearly every way from the older, rural communities in California.

The high occupational and educational achievement is reflected in the percentage of immigrants who arrive already possessing considerable skills.

TABLE 2

OCCUPATIONAL STATUS OF ARRIVING ASIAN INDIAN IMMIGRANTS[19] JUNE 1974 - JUNE 1975

Total	**15,773**	
Professional, Technical and Kindred Workers	6,157	(39%)
Managers and Administrators, except farm	481	(3%)
Housewives, Children & others with no occupation reported	7,763	(49%)
Other categories*	1,373	(8.7%)

* including some 150 farm-related occupational declarations

Such relatively large numbers in so short a time, coupled with their above average training, radically changed the social composition of South Asians in the U.S. and had similar effects on the demographic distribution. Into the late 1950's and early 1960's, the Asian Indians in the U.S. could have been divided into two groups, the rural, largely Punjabi Sikh Asian Indians in California, and the mixed Hindu, Sikh, Moslem urbanites of the urban areas on the East and West coasts and in the Mid-West. By 1966, this was changing and by 1970 it was evident that even in California, the number of urban Hindu and Indian Moslem segments were larger than the rural Sikh population. The West Coast, which had been *the* one major center of Sikh immigration, remained an important destination, but not the only one.

Alien address reports show a clear clustering, less than a dozen states having large resident alien populations. As of 1975 immigrants of *all* origins chose California over all other states (1,129,706) followed by New York (794,508), Florida (371,114), and Texas (327,668). A large number of Asian Indians presently chose (as do many migrants) to live either in California or the East Coast. Census figures substantiate this in a number of areas. The Alien Address program results for fifteen states were examined (Table 3) for 1975.

TABLE 3

REPORTED RESIDENCE OF ASIAN INDIANS ON PERMANENT STATUS BY SELECTED STATES FOR THE YEAR JUNE 1974-JUNE 1975[20]

Total	75,847	
New York	15,471	(20%)
Illinois	8,622	(11%)
New Jersey	8,481	(11%)
California	8,406	(11%)
Pennsylvania	4,385	(6%)
Ohio	3,572	(5%)
Michigan	3,561	(5%)
Maryland	2,971	(4%)
Texas	2,700	(3%)
Massachusetts	2,249	(3%)
West Virginia	1,436	(2%)
Connecticut	1,347	(2%)
All other States	12,646	(17%)

Additional confirmation comes from the initial choice of residence by arriving Asian Indian migrants. Table 4 shows those figures of 1975 and 1976.

TABLE 4

CHOICE OF RESIDENCE BY ASIAN INDIAN IMMIGRANTS BY SELECTED STATES JUNE 1974 - JUNE 1976[21]

	1974 - 75		1975 - 76	
Total	15,773	(100%)	17,487	(100%)
New York	3,992	(25.3%)	3,683	(21%)
Illinois	1,996	(12.6%)	2,755	(15.7%)
California	1,784	(11.4%)	2,065	(11.8%)
New Jersey	1,374	(8.7%)	1,453	(8.3%)
	9,146	(58.0%)	9,956	(56.8%)

As Tables 3 and 4 show, New York has received the largest percentage for any state as both a choice for arriving immigrants and place-of-residence for Asian Indians on permanent status. California reports about half of the New York figures, accounting for about 10% of the current total U.S. Asian Indian immigration. The immigrants are as unevenly distributed *within* the states as they are among the states. For example, in 1975, 1,884 Asian Indian immigrants took up residence in California.

TABLE 5

DISTRIBUTION OF ASIAN INDIAN IMMIGRANTS BY REPORTED RESIDENCE IN CALIFORNIA FOR THE YEAR JUNE 1974 - JUNE 1975[23]

Total - 1,884				
A)	Under 2,500 inhabitants (rural)			2
B)	2,500 - 99,000 inhabitants (urban)			1,142
C)	Selected Cities (over 100,000)			
	Northern area:			
	Berkeley	35		
	Fremont	3		
	Oakland	77		
	San Francisco	208		
	San Jose	37	420	
	Sacramento	29		
	Stockton	9		
	Fresno	22		
	Southern area:			
	Glendale	4		
	Anaheim	11		
	Los Angeles	207		
	Long Beach	18	310	
	Pasadena	27		
	Torrence	5		
	Santa Ana	3		
	San Diego	35		730
No report				1
All others				9
Total				1,884

A special 'Third World' Population in California census, estimated that the Asian Indian population as a whole increased from 13,410 in 1970 to 30,000 in 1977, a jump of 124%![22] Table 5 shows the distribution for 1975.

The figures in Table 5 show a rough sixty-forty split for 1974-75 in the urban areas between the greater Bay area in the north and greater metropolitan Los Angeles in the south. Location of the remainder is not specifically identified in the census reports, but those nearly 1,200 migrants who constitute 64% of the states' Asian Indian total are rather evenly divided between those who live in smaller urban/suburban areas such as Los Altos Hills or Modesto and those who live in the agricultural centers such as Yuba City/Marysville. My estimate of new arrivals in Yuba City/Marysville in the years 1972-1975 was close to 500 per year.[24] This would correlate with census estimates for non-specified urban locations (64%), allowing 500 immigrants per year into the bi-county area (41% of the "urban" category or a little over 25% of the *total* Asian Indian immigration into California), the remainder accounted for by the populations in settlements in the smaller central valley towns. This indicates that the growth rate for the Yuba City Sikh community over the past decade has been as high as 30% per year and was at least 10% in 1975.

What is important is not simply the physical growth but the social characteristics of the new population infusion and the effect of this immigration, both on the incoming groups and upon the already existing Sikh community. The physical growth of the Northern Sacramento Valley and its impact on a revitalized sense of community can be quantitatively seen in Table 6.

TABLE 6
ASIAN INDIAN POPULATION ESITIMATES
AND SOURCES FOR
YUBA CITY-MARYSVILLE AREA 1948-1974[25]

Source	Period	Population
Miller, 1950	Summer 1948	350-400
Jacoby, 1955	1954	300
Wenzel, 1966	1965	700-750
LaBrack, 1975	1974-1975	3800-4000+
California, 1977	1977	4500
Gibson, 1979	1980	6000
LaBrack, 1981	1981	6200+

By the late 1970's the population of the Sikh agricultural community of Yuba City/Marysville contained at least four times as many people as the entire Asian Indian population of the U.S. in 1947.

In place of the relatively landless laboring class was a fairly wealthy owner-operator group of Sikhs who owned (as of 1976) over 7,000 acres of prime orchard crop land and whose members were entering mercantile, white collar, professional, and educational fields in increasing numbers. The economic relationship between peach and other labor intensive field crops and the Sikhs is a complex one which I have dealt with more extensively elsewhere,[26] but for the purposes of illustrating cultural change it is sufficient to say that it provided the economic and residential base for sponsoring the immigration of large numbers of relatives and friends. The educational level has steadily increased and few Sikhs fail to graduate from high school, many going on to junior college and university degrees. The cultural decline so evident in the period up to 1947 has been reversed and many customs long out of practice or which have been impossible to maintain have reappeared, including arranged marriage, endogamy, and traditional religious observances. There are three active *gurdwaras* in the area, the first built in 1967 (the first one in California was built in Stockton in 1912). Punjabi food, language, and dress are generally followed in the home and all the indices related to a reestablishment of traditional Sikh life are on the increase. In many ways there has been a revitalization of Asian Indian lifestyle to an extent which most observers of the community in 1947 would have thought impossible. Communication between the Punjab homeland of the Sikhs and California is active, both in terms of frequent travel back and forth and informationally. Moreover, there is contact with other overseas centers of Sikh life, such as England, Fiji, East Africa and even New Zealand. The Canadian Sikh centers such as Vancouver, British Columbia, Toronto, Montreal, and Winnipeg maintain close ties, including frequent marriage between Canadian and U.S. Sikhs.

Not all Sikh communities are as contiguous or homogeneous as the Yuba City Sikhs nor are most in California rural. The Los Angeles and

San Francisco Bay areas have large and active Sikh groups and have recently built new gurdwaras in both areas. What *is* a common feature of immigrant Sikhs is their desire to maintain the integrity of their socio-religious system while pursuing a place in the American political and economic arena. The Immigration Act of 1965 and subsequent legislation have done more than simply allow the physical renewal of a people legally discriminated against for three decades. It has made possible resurgence in their culture, much like that sought and celebrated by many ethnic groups since the late 1960's. Their progress, both in economic terms and in maintaining their culture is remarkable.[27] A study of the immigration laws themselves shows only what is permissible and possible. For the Sikhs of California and many other Asian Indian groups (the Gujarati Patels for example) the opening of immigration represented a great opportunity, one which they have been quick to take advantage of.[28] In the process a once quickly disappearing minority group has become one of the fastest growing immigrant populations in the nation and one of its most successful.

FOOTNOTES

*   Bruce La Brack, Ph.D. is Associate Professor of Anthropology and International Studies at the University of the Pacific, Stockton, California 95211.

1.   This article is based in part upon materials collected between 1974 and 1980, including a field-investigation of eighteen months in 1974-75. Research was made possible through grants from the National Science Foundation and support from Syracuse University in the form of a Maxwell Fellowship and a supplementary research grant from the South Asia Program. Continuing research has been supported in part by Faculty Research Grants from the University of the Pacific (1976, 1977, 1978, 1980, 1981) and the Asian-American Program of the University of California-Davis. Portions of this data are drawn from Chapter VI of my dissertation, *The Sikhs of Northern California,* Particularly the material on post-1965 immigration.

2.   Jacoby, Harold S. *A Half-Century Appraisal of the East Indians in the United States.* Stockton: University of the Pacific. 1956.

3.   Preliminary estimate obtained through the Federal Information Center, Sacramento, California, October 22, 1981.

4.   Background to the 1909 exclusion is available in two 1908 reports by W.L. Mackenzie King to the Canadian government. *Report on Mission to England to Confer with the British Authorities on the Subject of Immigration to Canada from the Orient and Immigration from India in Particular;* and, *Report of the Royal Commission Appointed to Inquire into the Methods by Which Oriental Laborers Have Been Induced to Come to Canada,* Ottawa, Canada. Also see Eric Wilton Morse, *Immigration and Status of British East Indians in Canada.* M.A.: Queens University, Ontario, 1936.

5.   The legal and social issues behind the 1917 Act can be seen in the 1914 House *Hearing on Restriction of Immigration of Hindu Laborers* 63rd Congress, 2nd session, Washington, D.C. 1914.

6.   The figure of 3000 is considered by some scholars to be a conservative estimate, although the covert nature of the immigration renders any estimate open to question. The bulk of these illegals entered, through Mexico, many having come via the Panama Canal. The majority of the Sikhs moved north but some settled in the El Centro area.

7.   These figures are for the years 1907-1947, the period of greatest immigration. It is doubtful that even this seemingly high ratio is accurate. Jacoby (1956) learned of only seven women on the west coast up to W.W. I and my research was unable to expand the list, most of the long-time residents confirming the fact that there were no more than a dozen Asian Indian women in California prior to W.W. II.

8.   Professor Joan M. Jensen argues in *Federal Policy in the Shaping of Indian Occupations in the United States,* (an unpublished 1974 paper) that government 'channeling' was largely responsible for the rural employment of early Asian Indians. I agree that some external pressure was present, but contend that many immigrants were traditionally peasant farmers and field work was culturally compatible with their backgrounds.

9.   The article by Yusuf Dadabhay, "Circuitous Assimilation Among Rural Hindustanis in California," *Social Forces,* 33 (Dec. 1954) pp. 138-141, is one of the few sources of published material on the so called half and half's. See also chapter IV, "The Mexican Interlude: Intermarriage and Cultural Compatability," in my Ph.D. dissertation, La Brack, Bruce. *The Sikhs of Northern California,* Syracuse University, 1980.

10.   Although signed on July 2 by President Truman, immigration did not actually begin until 1947.

11.   U.S. Department of Commerce, Bureau of Census, *Sixteenth Census of the United States, 1940 — Population; Characteristics of the Nonwhite Population by Race.* Washington, D.C. 1943, 2-7, 17, 34, 37. For an excellent summary of the legal issues to 1946 see: Hess, Gary R. "The 'Hindu' in America," *Pacific Historical Review,* 31:1 (Feb.), 1961, 59-79 as well as his "The East Indian Community in the United States," *Pacific Historical Review* 63:4 (November), 1974, 576-596.

12. Carey McWilliams' book *Factories In the Field* (Boston: Little, Brown 1939), recounts the successive use of immigrant minority groups as field labor, "Hindus" are mentioned in Chapter 16 (p. 103-133). Also see his *Brothers Under the Skin* (New York: Little, Brown 1964) (revised), pages 248-249.

13. For statistics on family composition and offspring to 1950 I am indebted to Harold Jacoby both for our many stimulating conversations on this topic and for his allowing me to read and utilize his unpublished manuscript, *East Indians in the United States: The First Half-Century.*

14. Data drawn from *Annual Reports* of the Census Bureau 1947 through 1975 and adjusted for category changes or political events (Partition, creation of Bangladesh) where possible.

15. Signed under President Johnson, the bill was actually formulated under John F. Kennedy's instigation and carried through under the subsequent administration.

16. See Roger Daniels' excellent article, "American Historians and East Asian Immigrants," *Pacific Historical Review,* 63: 4 (November) 1974, pp. 449-472.

17. U.S. Department of Commerce, *Statistical Abstract of the United States,* 1975, (Washington, D.C.)

18. Estimate of 1975 East Indian population from Indian Embassy, Washington D.C. Correspondence of March 18, 1975.

19. Adapted from Table 34, "Immigrants Admitted by Country or Region of Birth and Major Occupational Group," U.S. Department of Justice, Immigration and Naturalization Service, *Annual Report* 1975. (Washington D.C.: United States Government Printing Office, 1975: 44).

20. Adapted from Table 12, "Aliens Who Reported Under the Alien Address Program by Selected Nationalities and State of Residence," U.S. Department of Justice, Immigration and Naturalization Services, *Annual Report, 1975.* Washington, D.C.: U.S. Government Printing Office 1975: 110-116. Initial 1980 census breakdowns by state show a continuation of population clustering. The largest Asian Indian components are found in New York (60,511), California (57,989), Illinois (35,711), and New Jersey (29,507). The Northeast region has 33% of the Asian Indians in the U.S. while the West Coast has 20%, the bulk of which is centered in the urban metropolitan areas of Los Angeles and the San Francisco Bay region.

21. Apapted from "Immigrants Admitted By Specified Countries of Birth and Rural and Urban Area and City," tables of U.S. Immigration and Naturalization Services, *Annual Reports of 1975 and 1976.*

22. *Third World Population in California.* Office of Lieutenant Governor, Council on Intergroup Relations, Intern Research Project, Sacramento, California. 1977: 4.

23. See note 21.

24. La Brack, Bruce. *Field Notes: Bi-County Sikh Population 1970-1975.*

25. Population data on Asian Indians is not as detailed or as accurate as researchers would desire; however, there are a number of sources for the 1947-1981 periods in the Yuba City area. Chronologically they are:

    1947 — Miller, Allen P. *An Ethnographic Report on the Sikh (East) Indians of the Sacramento Valley.* Mss. University of California-Berkeley, 1950: p. 8.

    1950 — Jacoby, Harold S. *A Half-Century Appraisal of East Indians in the United States.* University of the Pacific, Faculty Research Lecture, May 28,1956, Stockton, California, 1956: p. 28.

    1965 — Wenzel, Lawrence A. *The Identification and Analysis of Certain Value Orientations of Two Generations of East Indians in California.* Ph.D.:University of the Pacific, 1966: p. 8.

    1975 — La Brack, Bruce. *Field Notes: Bi-County Sikh Population — 1970-1975.*

    1976 — *Third World Population in California.* Office of Lieutenant Governor, Council on Intergroup Relations, Intern Research Project, Sacramento,CA, 1977: p. 4.

    1979 — Personal correspondence with Dr. Margaret Gibson, Co-Director of National Institute of Education project currently being conducted in theYuba City area.

    1981 — La Brack, Bruce. *Field Notes: Census Update 1981.*

26. La Brack, Bruce, *Occupational Specialization Among California Sikhs.* Paper delivered at Fifth Punjab Studies Conference, March 21-23, 1975, Berkeley, California. A revised and expanded version of this paper will appear in *Amerasia Journal* in 1982.

27. A recent study by Maxine P. Fisher, *The Indian of New York City* (Columbia, Missouri, South Asia Books, 1980) outlines the professional, educated nature of this Asian Indian urban group. Another by A.W. Helweg, *Sikhs in England* (Delhi: Oxford University Press, 1979), illustrates cultural continuity and identity maintenance in the face of social discrimination and legal barriers in another overseas Sikh community.

28. Jain, Usha R. *The Gujaratis of San Francisco,* M.A. Thesis: University of California-Berkeley 1964.

Marriage and Family Life Among Early Asian Indian Immigrants

Karen Leonard*

A recent issue of *India-West* presented the biography of one of the Sikh pioneers in California, a man who remained single in this country. The final paragraph commented: "To counter loneliness and to gain the rights of property-ownership he did not, like many others, remarry Mexican girls here . . . [he is admired for] not for a moment forgetting his commitment to his family."[1] The tone is bitter and the charge is explicit. One wonders just how many Asian Indian men did marry here, and how those marriages affected relationships among the immigrants from India and between them and their relatives in India.

The research previously published gives few insights into these fascinating issues. Without exception, the marriages of the early Asian Indians here have been underenumerated.[2] Only Yusuf Dadabhay in his well-known 1954 article on "circuitous assimilation" ventured to suggest the major role marriages with Mexican women played for many immigrants from India, and important parts of his argument have proved incorrect.[3]

The following report on research in progress focuses on men from India who farmed and married in California in the early decades of this century.[4] Their marriages and family life constitute an important part of the history of Asian Indians in the United States; they are also important to the history of ethnicity in the United States.

Asian Indian men began arriving in the U.S. in 1904. Viewed from India, their employment overseas was a family strategy which helped prospering Punjabi farmers adapt to the rising population density and prevent detrimental subdivision of land among the greater numbers of surviving sons. One son was sent out to earn money, as a policeman in Shanghai or Hong Kong, or as a laborer or farm worker in Australia, parts of Africa, Canada, or California. The money sent home helped support his patrilineage, the landholding and work unit among farming classes in the Punjab.

Given the early age at marriage in the Punjab at the time, it is probable that most of the men working overseas were married. They intended to return to India periodically or to send for their families after securing land here; only a handful took their wives along. But discriminatory laws passed in the U.S. from 1917 barred further immigration by Asians, and the choices the men faced were hard. They could stay and send the needed money home, but they could not bring their families. If they returned to India, they could not legally reenter the United States. If they reentered illegally, they would always be subject to arrest and deportation.

Other discriminatory legislation, aimed at preventing Japanese and other Asians from becoming citizens and landowners, was explicitly applied to Asian Indians from 1923[5], slowing the transition they were making from laborer to landowner in several regions of California.[6] In addition, miscegenation laws existed in California, as in most states, with varying provisions and degrees of enforcement. The racial categorization of Asian Indians was in practice a matter for local discretion, left to the whim of county clerks. All of these constraints were important factors for the immigrants who stayed in the United States, and they worked with them and around them in several ways.

For many years these immigrants did not marry in the U.S. The Immigration Commission's survey of 474 Asian Indians in 1909 included a table on marital status and location of wife: 31 of the men were widowed, 228 were single, and 215 were married. All 215 wives were abroad, back in India.[7] Some of these men had been in the U.S. for five years, but no local marriages had yet occurred.

The first recorded marriage I have found took

place in 1916 in the Imperial Valley, California's newly-developed agricultural valley bordering Mexico on the extreme southeast of the state.[8] The southern California base of marriage and family life for the men from India is illustrated by the following table and map. Compiled from county records of Sikh marriages and births and statewide records of Sikh deaths, the table indicates Asian Indian settlement and work patterns by 1940 in California (remember that Sikhs were at least 85% of these immigrants). Note that the births, marriages[9], and deaths of women over 18 (wives) and of children under 18 are concentrated in the Imperial Valley, with a small cluster in Fresno at the southern end of the San Joaquin Valley. (The deaths of the men are correlated with counties of work, not settlement, and the highest figures are in the northern and central San Joaquin Valley rather than the Imperial Valley.)

TABLE I
SIKH VITAL STATISTICS, 1905-1939

County	Births	Marriages	Deaths		
			Children	Women	Men ****
Imperial	183	16	29	2	36
Fresno*	38	6	3	3	61
San Joaquin	12	3	3	0	90
Sutter	7	1	0	0	26
Sacramento	5	4	4	1	53
Yuba	2	0	2	0	41
San Diego	**	10***	2	1	3
Los Angeles	n.a.	4	0	1	17
San Bernardino	—	—	2	0	7
Placer	—	—	2	0	25
Butte	—	—	1	0	9
Tulare	—	—	1	0	13
Kings	—	—	0	1	2
San Francisco	—	—	0	0	14
Contra Costa	—	—	0	0	10
Glenn	—	—	0	0	6
Yuma, Arizona	—	20	—	—	—

   * Singhs only checked so far.
  ** Research still to be done.
 *** This figure comes from the 25 divorce cases filed in Imperial County befor 1940. Those marriages were performed in the following places: San Diego, 10; El Paso, Texas, 5; Arizona, 5; Los Angeles, 3; New Mexico, 1; unknown, 1.
**** 5 or fewer deaths of Sikh men are recorded in 12 other counties before 1939; I have not included these counties in the table.

COUNTIES, 1974

-N-

0 20 40 60 80 100
miles

Historical Atlas of California, 1978

The question that one wants to answer is — why did the men marry, and why did the men in the south marry more? The alien land law was clearly applied to Asian Indians following the 1923 Thind decision depriving them of eligibility for citizenship, and it has been alleged that they married to secure land, thay they used their wives and their children to lease and own land for them. One way of checking is by looking at the women's birthplaces: does there seem to be a preference for spouses born in the U.S., who were automatically U.S. citizens, after 1923?

There are some difficulties with this as a test, the major one being that married women legally were held to have assumed the citizenship of their husbands (until 1931-32). But this was a hotly disputed question during the 1920's.[10] Another difficulty here is that Mexican-born persons could of course become citizens, and it is possible that many of the wives did so. But most of these earliest spouses, chiefly born between 1882 and 1910, were illiterate; I have yet to check the Naturalization records at every level, but so far I have found only one Mexican-born wife who became a U.S. citizen, and she did so in 1954.[11] The third difficulty is that, in practice, both women born in Mexico and their Asian Indian husbands appear to have entered into leasing and ownership relationships, cetainly verbal and even recorded ones, in Imperial County despite the law until the 1930's.

In any case, let us examine 253 couples formed by 1947, dividing them into those relationships formed before 1924 and those formed in and after 1924, when the prohibition on Asian land-leasing and ownership became effective. Omitting the women for whom I have no birthplace information (4 before 1924 and 40 afterward), the percentage of the pre-1924 spouses born in Mexico was 50%; after 1924, that percent rose to 53%. 42% of the pre-1924 spouses were born in the U.S.; after 1924, that percentage rose to 47%. (It is the five Indian wives who constitute the other 8% before 1924.) We see, then, no significant change in marriage preferences caused by the 1923 legal change.[12]

What about the children as possible motivation for the marriages? Certainly many were born to these couples, most on the U.S. side of the border, and perhaps land was leased and bought in their names. I checked the probate records to see when fathers began to register as guardians, that is, when they put land legally in their children's names. In the Imperial Valley, this practice began only in 1933 and 1934 — the obvious stimulus here was the 1933 Grand Jury indictment of some 65 Asian Indians and others for "conspiracy to evade the alien land law."[13]

From the above, it is perfectly clear that the men from India did not marry in order to hold leases and/or land in the names of their wives and children. This was sometimes done, of course[14], but it was not the motive for the large numbers of marriages with Hispanic women in southern California.

An analysis of these first 73 couples, those recorded in California *before* 1924, shows several characteristic patterns. In the Imperial Valley, 60 men had settled down: 52 of the women were Hispanic, 5 were Anglo, and 3 were black.[15] The 52 Hispanic wives included 15 sets of related women, involving 31 of these wives.[16] In Fresno, 5 men had married: there were 4 Hispanic wives (including one set of 3 sisters) and one Asian Indian wife. In Stockton and Sacramento, there were 2 couples each, and all four wives were Asian Indian (although one had been born in Canada). In the Yuba/Sutter area, there were 4 couples: two wives were Hispanic, one was Anglo, and one was Asian Indian.

Thus in the south, the Imperial Valley and Fresno, the women were almost all Hispanic. In the north, there were very few couples before 1924, and five of the eight wives were Asian Indian. These regional and ethnic differences persisted, as summarized in the table below.

Quantitatively, this is a small community; it is the qualitative aspects of these marriages which are fascinating. The men who worked and settled together, although seldom related by blood, were frequently village mates from the same or nearby villages in the Punjab, had served together in the British Army or Police, or had been shipmates on the way to America. They formed partnerships to pool their capital and labor, leasing land in groups of two to five men, with the one who knew English best acting as agent. They did not marry until years after arriving in America, until the immigration laws made it impossible to bring their families from India, so they were all in their 30's and 40's when they married, and their wives were usually much

TABLE II
ETHNICITY AND COUNTY OF WIVES

	Imperial	Fresno	Yuba/Sutter	San Joaquin	Sacramento	Total
Before 1924	60: 52 H 5 W 3 B	5: 4 H 1 I	4: 2 H 1 I 1 W	2: 2 I	2: 2 I	73
1924-1947	129: 122 H 7 W	21: 16 H 5 W	21: 12 H 7 W 1 B 1 AI	6: 4 H 1 W 1 I	3: 2 H 1 I	180
Totals	189	26	25	8	5	253

H = Hispanic   I = Asian Indian   W = White   B = Black   AI = American Indian

Source: family reconstitution from county records, 6 counties above.

younger. In the Imperial Valley, partners lived together on the land they were farming, and, when one married, his wife moved into that joint household.

As discussed above, the Asian Indians tended to marry sisters, or sets of related women and the men were often linked as partners too. The first three Asian Indian/Hispanic marriages in the Imperial Valley were those of the Alvarez sisters, who married Sikhs in 1916 and 1917, and two of the three husbands were partners. Thus, kinship and economic ties reinforced each other, in this and many other such instances.

It is fairly clear that, for the Asian Indian men, these marriages with Hispanic women offered little in the way of economic resources. Very few Mexicans leased or owned land in the Imperial Valley then (or now). The decision to marry here rested on a realistic assessment of the men's legal predicament, the economic cost of voyages to and from India coupled with the dangers of illegal reentry, and the relative success experienced by many Asian Indian farmers in the second decade of the century. Some were forming stable leasing arrangements, buying land, entering into ongoing relationships with bankers, shippers and processors, merchants, and so on in their areas of settlement.[17] In the south, Spanish-speaking women were available, and legal barriers to such marriages were not raised.[18] The women offered domesticity; a housekeeper and cook for the husband and for his partners; and children.

For these Hispanic women from Mexico and the American southwest, the marriages to Asian Indians seem to have been a step up. Many were themselves migrant laborers, moving with their families as part of the flood of Mexican labor entering California's agricultural industry in the second decade of this century.[19] Others came from families displaced by the Mexican Revolution and the disorganization along the border from Texas to California. Often the sets of sisters, or mother and daughters, who married Asian Indians lacked male relatives.[20] The women were young, as much as 20 years younger than their husbands, and if they were past their teens they had usually been married before and brought young children into the marriage. Most of the women marrying Asian Indians came from female-centered, lower-class Mexican kinship groups.

The marriage network in that first decade after 1915 was wide-ranging in two ways. First, it often linked Asian Indians of Muslim, Sikh, and Hindu religious persuasion through their (Hispanic) wives, a situation most unlike that in the Punjab. Not only the marriages themselves, but the two witnesses signing for each ceremony show the Punjabi regional and linguistic, rather than religious, basis of community among the early immigrants. The men formed a Hindustani

Association in the Imperial Valley, partly to coordinate farming interests and partly to mediate conflicts among themselves,[21] and there were a few partnerships formed across religious lines.

Second, the marriage network was geographically wide, including men and women from Canada, Mexico, Texas, Utah, New Mexico, Arizona, and California. Once one Hispanic woman married an Asian Indian, she was likely to introduce her sisters, mother, or cousins to other Asian Indian men, friends of her husband. Men living in Marysville in northern California journeyed to Fresno or the Imperial Valley, where a friend introduced them to an eligible woman. If not arranged marriages in the Indian sense, many of the early marriages were certainly marriages by referral.

The Hispanic wives introduced problems as well: a female-centered kinship network; Spanish, not Punjabi or English as a home language; an age difference, Catholicism, to the extent that it was practiced; and an orientation towards a subculture in California which was identified with the migrant laborer class, not the farmer class. This subculture had a lower status in both Punjabi and Anglo value systems.[22] Potentially even more unsettling to the men, the women could threaten income and property. The first few divorce cases must have been a shock to the Punjabi farmers, as their wives successfully petitioned for division of community property, child support, and alimony. At that time in India (1919 was the first case filed in the Imperial County), legal provisions for divorce and compensation were not available to women.[23]

These marriages were not conflict-free, and there was frequent practice of serial monogamy, chiefly as a result of divorce.[24] In my first attempt to list the men and women married more than once, using an early Imperial Valley list of some 130 couples, I found that 35 of the men and 47 of the women had married more than once. The divorce ratio was high for the time, and it also ran counter to general trends showing a lower ratio of divorces for rural, foreign-born, and Catholic persons.[25]

The men and women filed in almost equal proportions for divorce, in the counties where I have looked at these records, and granted that the petitions were overstated to meet the re-

quirements of the day, they still make interesting reading. According to the men's petitions, the women refused to carry out the duties of marriage. They argued with their husbands, cursed them, and refused to clean and cook for their husbands' friends. They insisted upon visiting their mothers and sisters when they wished, went to town to shop, and liked to buy and use makeup. They demanded medical care for female complaints and confinements. They enjoyed dancing and generally stepping out with male, usually Mexican, friends. According to the women, their Asian Indian husbands tended to drink, beat them, commit adultery, and demand domestic services beyond reason, while refusing household and medical essentials. Verbal abuse, including racial slurs, and physical violence, drinking and adultery, were reported by most petitioners of both sexes. Both fathers and mothers wanted custody of the children, if there were any — in contrast to most of the marriages, which produced many children, the couples who divorced tended to have few or no children.[26]

Many of the men's partnerships also ended in legal disputes. Literally dozens of legal cases, mostly against each other, were filed by Asian Indians in their first years in Imperial County, showing a readiness to resort to the courts like that of their relatives in British India. The courts did not solve all the problems: the first three murders by Asian Indians in the Imperial Valley centered on partnerships (the first, in 1917), and the marital disputes involving a wife's Mexican relatives (1919 and 1921).[27]

To explain these marital and work conflicts, let us quickly summarize significant differences between Punjabi society and that of the Asian Indians in the Imperial Valley in the 1920's. Both were frontier areas based on irrigation agriculture,[28] but the structures of resource control and of marriage networks were quite different. Punjabi society was patriarchal, and the patrilineal joint family was the agricultural landholding and work unit. Arranged marriages were characterized by village exogamy and patrilocal residence, so that daughters left their homes and relatives at marriage while sons stayed in the parental home and continued to work the family land. In contrast, the marriage networks of Asian Indians in the Imperial Valley linked men through a Hispanic, lower-class, female-centered system, where a wife's mother and/or sisters were nearby (if not part of the household). This situation was coupled to a legal system barring Asians from direct control of land and providing for community property. The men's partnerships were not only based on ties more fragile than blood — village, regiment, ship, wives — but were divorced from landholding, or at least from secure landholding. If we add that the wives were many years younger than their husbands, and that the husbands regularly sent a good portion of their earnings back to India to family there, the fact that many of these marriages did survive and flourish becomes remarkable.

As the men married and settled on particular ranches in the Valley, social networks were constituted which were based on the men's partnerships and the women's female kin. The wives usually learned to cook a few special dishes — chicken curry, roti — and most understood a bit of Punjabi, since they lived for some years in joint households with their husbands' partners. Couples visited back and forth for dinner parties; they became godparents for each others' children.[29] The children were typically given Hispanic first names, were baptized Catholics, and spoke both Spanish and English at home. (Most were able to understand some Punjabi.) There were a great many single "uncles," bachelor partners and friends of their fathers, among whom the children distinguished by making up Spanish nicknames or by using the village and clan tags their fathers employed for the same purpose.[30] Although the fathers retained their religious affiliations, to Sikhism, Islam, or Hinduism, seldom did the women or children have more than the vaguest idea about that religion.[31] There was no Sikh temple in El Centro until 1946 (when the men purchased the Buddhist temple left after the Japanese were taken away from the Valley), and the Sikh temple in Stockton was a long drive.[32] Few spouses converted to the other's religion: there is one instance of a wife becoming a Muslim, and one of a husband becoming a Catholic. There are several instances of a Sikh or Muslim husband going through a Catholic marriage ceremony so that the wife could continue to take communion in her church.[33] The children, while often respectful of

their father's culture and curious about it, had immediate access only to their mother's culture. So pervasive was the Mexican-American subculture among the Asian Indians that the daughter of one of the handful of Anglo wives of Asian Indians in the Imperial Valley in the 1920's observed that her family had been quite isolated from the other Asian Indian families because her mother had not known Spanish.

My historical reconstitution of the Asian Indian families established in California shows that Dadabhay was correct about the fundamental orientation of early Asian Indian marriage and family networks toward the Mexican-American subculture. This Mexican-Asian Indian population cannot be termed an ethnic subsystem in its own right,[34] but the Mexican-Asian Indians have *not* entirely merged into the Mexican-American subculture as Dadabhay predicted. Identification with Mexican-American culture did not provide resources helpful to the Asian Indian immigrants in their quest to become successful farmers in California, and their descendants who are in farming retain the term "Hindu" as an ethnic label.

Actual ties with relatives in India vary a good deal depending on family circumstances and individual attitudes. Most of the men, although married here, continued to send money back to their families and relatives in the Punjab, as I have heard from many of their Hispanic widows and children. While sometimes this clearly had been a divisive factor in family relationships in the U.S., it was usually considered a family obligation and one to be honored. Some Hispanic wives, and more of the Mexican-Asian Indian children, eventually visited India and met the relatives to whose welfare they had contributed over the years. Children born here have travelled to India to meet their half-brothers and half-sisters. In one case, it was a son here who worried about his half-brother's welfare, initiated contact, and persuaded his father and brothers to send money to the Punjabi family. Children here are proud of their fathers for their economic contributions not only to relatives but to their villages; there are many cases of the men designating funds for schools to be built in their home villages. There are also instances of suspicion and distrust, where descendants fend off contacts with India, fearing claims on their property and resources here. This attitude is more common in the south, which helps to explain the sharp regional contrasts which exist in California today.

Thus the Sikh ethnic community reconstituted in the north is based on the male ethnic population, which persisted until Sikh women could be brought over. In the northern twin cities of Yuba City/Marysville the Punjabi language is flourishing. The fewer than one thousand Sikhs of the 1960's have become at least 6,000 strong; endogamy is strictly adhered to, with marriages being arranged between U.S. and Indian born persons and many marriages taking place in India. Social controls according to caste, village, and region back in the Punjab are imposed in Yuba City.

In contrast to that, the Imperial Valley descendants of Asian Indians now the third and fourth generation, do not constitute a community; they are heterogeneous by class and culture. Only a handful of old men there are Sikhs, in terms of language, religion, and family life (three of them brought wives from India in the 1950's). Some persons descended from the Asian Indian immigrants report themselves as Mexican today; others claim to be "Hindu" but are unaware of the differences between Hindus, Muslims and Sikhs. Some Punjabis and their sons have done well and are leading members of the grower-banker establishment today; others continue as farm laborers or have gone into other service occupations in the Valley. But they are all proud of their "Hindu" ancestors, who were pioneers in every respect, including their personal life.

FOOTNOTES

*   Karen Leonard, Ph.D., Associate Professor, Department of Social Sciences, University of California, Irvine, CA 92717.

1.   Ramesh Murarka. "Pratap S. Brar," *India West,* July 13, 1981, 12-13.

2.   References to previous research can be found in Bruce La Brack's article in this issue. No one had systematically collected information on all Asian Indian marriages in California, although Harold Jacoby's data is good and accurately indicates the trends.

3.   Yusuf Dadabhay, "Circuitous Assimilation Among Rural Hindustanis in California," *Social Forces,* 33:2 (Dec., 1954), 138-141. Hindustanis have not assimilated to American culture by becoming Mexican-Americans, and the latter subculture did not particularly welcome them, as forthcoming work will show.

4.   This reasearch, funded by grants from the University of California, Irvine, is based upon family reconstitution of persons named Singh through collation of birth, marriage, and death certificates at county record offices. I have completely reconstituted families for the six counties of major settlement (Imperial, Yuba, Sutter, Fresno, Sacramento, and San Joaquin), adding 20 to 50 Sikh, Muslim, and Hindu surnames as my knowledge of families settled in each locality increased. To supplement those records, I am using statewide records which are centralized and on microfiche, as well as county records pertaining to land leasing and ownership, and civil and criminal cases (including probate).

5.   Harold S. Jacoby, "More Thind Against than Sinning," *The Pacific Historian,* 11:4 (Nov., 1958), 1-2, 8. (Bhagat Singh Thind was the appellant.)

6.   *California and the Oriental,* Report of the State Board of Control of California (Sacramento, 1922), 47-48.

7.   The Immigration Commission. *East Indians on the Pacific Coast* (1909), 338.

8.   This was the marriage of Sher Singh and Antonia Alvarez, in November of 1916.

9.   Couples from Imperial County frequently went to Yuma, Arizona, or to San Diego or Los Angeles for the civil marriage ceremony. This was apparently because of differential enforcement of the miscegenation law, or because Yuma from 1927 had no waiting period, or because it became a festive trip.

10.   Taraknath Das. "Stateless Persons in the U.S.A.," *The Calcutta Review,* 3rd series, 16:1 (July, 1925), 40-46.

11.   This was Luz/Lucy Harper Sekhon, now of San Diego (and of Irish-Mexican parentage): Laguna Niguel Federal Archives, naturalization petition no. 18893 of 1954.

12.   One might expect a lower percentage of Mexican-born spouses after 1924, as more Mexican-Americans were born in the U.S., but for these men the percentage of Mexican-born spouses increased slightly.

13.   J. Labh Singh et al were convicted in 1934 of conspiracy to evade the alien land laws (prison for the Asian Indians and fines for the Anglos): contemporary newspapers give details, in the collection of Joseph Anderholt for the Pioneers (Imperial County Historical Society). The first guardianship case was filed in 1929, followed by many others from 1934 on: Imperial County Probate Records, 1916-1949.

14. An early example is that of the lawyer, Sakharam Ganesh Pandit, who successfully appealed to retain his citizenship in 1923. His wife, a white woman and a citizen, owned property in the Imperial Valley: U.S. Senate, Committee on Immigration, "Ratification and Confirmation of Naturalization of Certain Persons of the Hindu Race," 69 Cong. 2 sess. (1926), 11.

15. The few black brides in the Imperial Valley were probably from families brought from the south to pick cotton around 1910: Paul S. Taylor, "Mexican Labor in the United States: Imperial Valley," University of California Publications in Economics, vol. 6 (1928), 6-7.

16. I have included here four women married before 1924 whose sisters later married Asian Indians.

17. Robert Higgs found that the duration of local residence was the most significant factor leading to "The Wealth of Japanese Tenant Farmers in California, 1909," in his airticle in *Agricultural History,* 53:2 (1979), 488-493. He reasoned that this was because of ties formed with bankers and merchants in the locality, and I think this would hold true for the Asian Indians as well.

18. See the demographic profiles (14th Census, 1920) in Allyn C. Loosley, "Foreign Born Population of California, 1919-1920," M.A. in. Economics, University of California, 1927. As for enforcement of the miscegenation law (on California's books until 1950), county clerks habitually described the Asian Indian men and women they were marrying in the same way, either "brown", "white," or "colored." The 1923 Thind decision had concluded that Asian Indians, although technically Caucasian, were not "white"; Mexicans were legally Caucasian and/or white, but they too were seldom so described until recently in California's county records. In 1933-34, Hispanic women suddenly began filing affidavits of "Indian ancestry" so that they and their Asian Indian marriage partners could both be described as "Indian" on the licenses, reflecting legal pressures against Asians no doubt connected with attempted enforcement of the land laws at that time.

19. Carey McWilliams points to 1908-25 as a time of turmoil along the border and he dates the big increase in Mexican immigration from 1917: *North from Mexico (1968),* 163, 111.

20. Interviews with the Spanish-speaking widows and their daughters: orphans, deserted women, a mother with her daughters moving from Mexico to El Paso, Los Angeles, El Centro . . . these were common stories.

21. Imperial County Index of Grantees, Book 7, page 211, where a Hindu's lease dated 7/16/19 includes the condition that a representative of the Hindustani Welfare and Reform Society can enter to inspect with the landlord (another Hindu). I owe this reference to Dr. Sucheng Chan, Ethnic Studies, University of California, Berkeley, who is working on Asian cultivators in California before 1924.

22. Most of the men were Jat Sikhs, a powerful farming caste in the Punjabi stratification system; there were only two untouchable Sikhs in the Imperial Valley.

23. Even now, with full legal provisions, under 1% of the Indian population has undergone legal divorce (1971 census).

24. For most I have two marriages recorded, although one man and one woman married five times, and one woman seven times. For the men, remarriages followed upon divorce and almost all spouses were Hispanic. For the women, some remarriages resulted from widowhood, and spouses included Mexican, Anglo, Sikh, Muslim, and Hindu men.

25. One consequence of these multiple marriages is a large number of step-children, some fathered by Mexicans or Anglos and raised by Sikh fathers, some fathered by Sikhs and raised by Mexican fathers, etc. Ties among half-siblings were apparently close, as can be inferred from the frequency with which half-siblings signed as witnesses to a marriage or birth (in the latter instance, filing affidavits for late birth certificates).

26. Imperial County Civil suits, 1910-1980, particularly the cases before 1940 (on microfilm in the County Clerk's office).

27. Imperial County Criminal cases, nos. 680 and 705; 1031; and 773 (on microfilm in the County Clerk's office).

28. The Punjab had centuries of historical experience in this way of life; the Imperial Valley was opened up after 1901, and the irrigation district began functioning dependably around 1910, after a stormy beginning.

29. Naming patterns changed over the decades, and individuals also used different forms of their names over the life cycle: Jaime/Jimmie, Juan/John, or Harbhajan/Harry are examples of birth to marriage changes. Some of the divorce cases featured parental conflict over the children's names; the Francisco and Emily whose custody a mother sought, for example, were really Baldev and Besenti, according to the father.

30. Inder Singh "Chuhra" (untouchable) was thus distinguished from Inder Singh "Charchukia" (from the village of Charchuk) or Inder Singh "chaparita" (whose wife was "the short one"), to give a fictitious example.

31. While there are exceptions to this generalization, the following are typical: one widow, who had lived with her Sikh husband 50 years (many of them in a joint household with his brother and two partners), referred to the "Singh" religion; another, a wife of 28 years to her husband, was unable to repeat correctly the customary Sikh greeting "sat sri akal."

32. This Stockton temple had been built in 1915 and remained the only one in California until 1946. Today, it is at least a 10-hour drive from the Imperial Valley.

33. These church ceremonies usually occurred many years after the first, civil, marriage, although I have two instances where a Sikh and a Muslim initially married their Mexican wives in Catholic ceremonies.

34. I will be publishing separately on this issue.

Asian Indian Americans: Search for an Economic Profile

by

Manoranjan Dutta*

I. Emergence of a New Viable Ethnic Group

"George, be a king!" Every mother may paraphrase it to say, "My child, be counted in the decennial census of the country where your tax dollars go." Thus, came the response of 361,544 immigrants of Asian Indian heritage as they filled up the 1980 census form of the United States.

This was the first U.S. census where they were categorically mentioned to be so counted. The 1980 census questionnaire in its question #4 asked for a specific response if the individual was an *Asian Indian*. The term race was abolished, and the question was rephrased. Along with terms, such as *White, Black, American Indian,* there were several specific categories referring to immigrants from Asian countries, — Japanese, Chinese, Filipino, Korean, Asian Indian, Vietnamese, and so on. The question thus referred to countries of origin whence the immigrant or his/her ancestors began their journey of immigration to the United States. Since categorization on the basis of race became a difficult, if not impossible task, categorization based on the source of immigration was the next best choice.

A very basic objective of the decennial census of population is to obtain a full and accurate enumeration of the people. If at all possible, there should be no undercount, or undercount must be held to the minimum. Studies of the 1970 decennial census of the United States established that there was an undercount of some two percent for the White population, and that the undercount for the Black was four times as high. Needless to say, efforts to minimize any undercount in the 1980 census became a prime target of the U.S. Bureau of the Census, and also of many concerned groups of citizens, especially the Black, the Hispanic, and the Asian/Pacific Americans.

For the Asian Indians, the initiative came as early as 1974 when the first representation was made to the U.S. Bureau of Census. The United States House of Representatives Subcommittee on Census and Population[2] received a delegation of Asian/Pacific American leadership at its hearings on June 1, 1976. This delegation was joined by the Asian Indians. The U.S. Bureau of the Census followed up by convening a conference of representatives of Asian/Pacific Americans. By July 1, 1976, the U.S. Secretary of Commerce, at the recommendation of the Director of the Bureau of the Census, appointed a statutory Advisory Committee for Asian/Pacific American Population for the 1980 Census. Indeed, this was the first and only statutory committee for Asian/Pacific Americans ever so appointed by the U.S. Government, and it worked through June 30, 1981, on the basis of bi-annual reappointments by successive Secretaries of the U.S. Department of Commerce, through three successive administrations. This Advisory Committee met twice a year and successfully developed recommendations covering all three phases of the 1980 census, first designing the questionnaire, second bringing inputs towards developing optimum field organization for the census operation, and finally suggesting procedures for the tabulation of the census findings.

In my view, the single most significant contribution made by the 1980 Census Advisory Committee for Asian/Pacific Americans related to the designing of the census questionnaire. There was a great deal of discussion and rather prolonged debate over a period of two years, should question four have been expanded to include so many Asian/Pacific categories. The one basic argument that finally proved to be convincing was simply the fact that even if the terms White and Black have historically received generic acceptance in the context of United States history, there hardly exists any such term to encompass immigrants and their children from different Asian countries and Pacific islands. As such, in the 1970 census specific mention was made for the four major categories: Japanese, Chinese, Korean and Filipino. Extension of the same format and its necessary expansion were considered the best way to encourage maximum responses of Asian/Pacific Americans to the 1980 census.

Specific mention of countries from which a sizeable group of immigrants arrived in the United States became the significant recommendation for maximizing responses of immigrants from various Asian countries to the 1980 census. It was then established that the number of Asian Indians in the United States in 1980 was expected to be so sizeable. The number of Korean population in 1970 became a benchmark to work with, since the category Korean was added as an independent category in the 1970 census questionnaire. The preliminary information base used for this exercise covered: (i) the 1970 census which gave a figure of some 70,000 Asian Indians, (ii) the U.S. Immigration and Naturalization Services which showed some 100,000 new immigrants from India, and (iii) sundry mark-up figures projecting natural growth of the 1970 figures and adding thereto number of immigrants from other countries including central America who would ethnically relate to the Asian Indian category. We projected a base number of 300,000 Asian Indians. Indeed, the final 1980 census figure is 361,000, and this Asian Indian figure is marginally larger than the number of immigrants from Korea. The present author appeared for the Asian/Pacific Advisory Committee before the U.S. Senate Subcommittee on Census and Population[4] and presented arguments to the group why specific mention of a group of countries was important to maximize responses of Asian/Pacific Americans. This smallest group of American population has to be encouraged to be responsive to the system. As of now there exists no generic term. It is not unlikely that at some future date, the generic term Asian/Pacific American will be accepted. In our mission to minimize undercount in the

decennial demographic census, any haste at this time to bring all immigrants and their children from various Asian countries and Pacific islanders under one such category must be counterproductive.

Two related issues need to be discussed. First, the term *Asian Indian* is significant. Could we use any other term such as, Indic, South Asian, East Indian, Hindusthani? The term *Indian* was considered the most precise for the response of the largest number of people in the category. Their response to the 1980 census was critical in terms of our basic goal, i.e. minimization of undercount for immigrants from the Indian subcontinent countries. We also searched for a term which would be commonly understood not only by the members of the specific group, but also by the rest of the people in the society. The term *Indian* of course met this test. Once we accepted the term Indian, a prefix or a suffix, *Asian,* became necessary. This would help preempt any possible confusion vis-à-vis the American Indian population. We respected their wishes in this regard. We also fulfilled the basic census goal of full enumeration of the group of population. Our recommendation for the term *Asian Indian* was finally adopted.

The second issue is if there is any serious undercount of the Asian Indian population in the 1980 census. "Undercount yes, serious no," has been my response. Some Asian Indians might have been misled to believe that they did not belong to the United States census, and that they must wait for the Indian decennial census. Given the educational-income profile, such mistakes cannot be a large scale happening. As for immigrants from other Indian subcontinent countries who will have checked the category *Others,* in the 1980 census form, the Bureau of the Census will use a sampling method to estimate the number of people immigrating here from each such country. The Bureau has agreed that once such estimates are completed, numbers for these groups, such as, Pakistani, Bangladeshi, Nepalese, Ceylonese, and so on will be published. Indeed, this same sampling method was used in the 1970 census to obtain the 70,000 figure for Asian Indians. Once such country-wise figures are established, scholars of

South Asian Studies will then be able to add up their regional totals, as may be suitable for their specific investigations.

II. The Regional Distribution of the Asian Indian Population

The 1980 census provides not only the U.S. national total of Asian Indian population, but also its regional distribution, state by state, and then county by county, as far as possible. The largest single concentration of the group is shown to be in the four-state region of New York-New Jersey-Connecticut-Pennsylvania. The four state total of 110,225 covers nearly a third of the total Asian Indian population.

Table 1
THE REGIONAL DISTRIBUTION

Region	Total	Percent
North East	120,761	33
North Central	85,119	24
South	83,586	23
West	72,078	20
Total	361,544	100

Note: North East includes New England (Maine, New Hampshire, Vermont, Massachusetts, Rhode Island, Connecticut) and Mid Atlantic States (New York, New Jersey and Pennsylvania). **North Central** consists of East North Central States (Ohio, Indiana, Illinois, Michigan, Wisconsin) and West North Central States (Minnesota, Iowa, Missouri, North Dakota, South Dakota, Nebraska, Kansas). **South** includes South Atlantic States (Delaware, Maryland, District of Columbia, Virginia, West Virginia, North Carolina, South Carolina, Georgia and Florida) plus East South Central States (Kentucky, Tennessee, Alabama, Mississippi) and West South Central States (Arkansas, Louisiana, Oklahoma, Texas). **West** includes Mountain States (Montana, Idaho, Wyoming, Colorado, New Mexico, Arizona, Utah, Nevada) and Pacific States (Washington, Oregon, California, Alaska and Hawaii).

Table 1 indicates that there is a fairly even distribution of the Asian Indian population across the four regions of the country, with a marginal tilt for the North East. A clearer view can be obtained if we look at the demographic map in groups of states in terms of Asian Indian population sizes, and in Table 2, we present such a picture.

For many and varied purposes relative to ethnic statistical compilation, the U.S. Govern-

Table 2
GROUPS OF STATES WITH VARYING SIZES OF ASIAN INDIAN POPULATION

Five States With 20,000 and more		Six States With 4,000 - 5,000	
New York	60,511	Connecticut	4,995
California	57,989	North Carolina	4,718
Illinois	35,711	Georgia	4,347
New Jersey	29,507	Indiana	4,290
Texas	22,226	Missouri	4,099
Four States With 13,000 - 15,000		Washington	4,002
Pennsylvania	15,212	**Five States With Least Concentration**	
Michigan	14,680	North Dakota	294
Maryland	13,705	Alaska	241
Ohio	13,105	South Dakota	182
Three States With 8,000 - 10,000		Wyoming	176
Florida	9,138	Montana	162
Virginia	8,483		
Massachusetts	8,387		

Source: The 1980 Census Report
The U.S. Bureau of the Census

ment follows the five-fold exhaustive classification of the American population — *White,* (who trace their ethnic origin to Europe), *Black* (who attribute their roots to Africa), Hispanic (who share their heritage with Central and South American countries), Asian/Pacific (who relate to the diverse old cultures of Asia) and the one non-immigrant group, *Natives of North America.* Asian Indians and others from the Indian subcontinent countries are included in the Asian/Pacific American Category. The 1980 census figures show that Asian Indians constitute a significant group in this specific category. Table 3 presents a summary of relative ranking of Asian Indians in terms of the total Asian/Pacific American population, and also in terms of several other major groups in the five selected states of major concentration of Asian Indian population.

Table 3
ASIAN/PACIFIC AMERICANS
AND ASIAN INDIANS

	Total	Asian Indian	Rank**
All United States*	3,500,638	361,544	4
New York	310,531	60,511	2
California	1,253,987	57,989	6
Illinois	159,551	35,711	2
New Jersey	103,842	29,507	1
Texas	120,306	22,226	3

Notes:
* According to the 1980 census figures, there are 6,756,986 *Others.* As and when the Bureau of the Census will have completed country-wide adjustments from this total, all those from various Asian countries will be added to the Asian/Pacific Total, and as such, the present total will be adjusted upward.

** The Rank of other preceding Asian/Pacific groups in order of their respective numerical sizes: All U.S. — Chinese (1), Filipino (2) and Japanese (3).
New York — Chinese (1); California — Filipino (1), Chinese (2), Japanese (3), Korean (4) and Vietnamese (5); Illinois — Filipino (1); Texas — Vietnamese (1) and Chinese (2)

Source: The 1980 Census Report
The Bureau of the Census

III. AN ECONOMIC PROFILE: MYTHS AND REALITIES

A definitive economic profile of Asian Indian Americans can be constructed only after a careful analysis of the 1980 census data, a mine of information on age-sex-occupation-education-income-house ownership, etc. Pending any such rigorous efforts, what we can provisionally offer must be based partly on intelligent guesses, and partly on occasional studies by concerned scholars. Most of these studies, however, are based on data which have not been gathered in terms of a well-defined statistical sampling design.

The family size of Asian Indians is believed to be relatively small. At one spectrum there are many single member units, while at another end there may be a few large familes. A fairly large number of them happen to be young immigrant couples with one child or just newly-wed. Let me suggest that on an average the family size of Asian Indians will be 3.6, much smaller than the standard size of five member families in most American demographic studies. Thus, one estimates that there are roughly 100,000 Asian Indian family units. Adjusting for single member units, we project that there are more than 200,000 Asian Indian adults in the American job market. The labor force participation rate of the group is much higher than the national average, and may be as high as 75 percent. This is judged to be so high because of the age-and-education pattern of Asian Indian immigrants. A very large number of them will be in the prime age group, between 25 and 55 years of age, and they have an above-average educational background. In addition, economic needs of a new immigrant family, coming as they do from a saving-poor country as India is, press both spouses to join the labor market. Even so, in the context of total American labor force of more than one hundred million, the absolute number of this group remains much too small.

If the absolute number poses no problem, there are other problems which one must carefully study before constructing an economic profile of Asian Indian Americans. The two general contributing factors one must recognize immediately are: First, some fifty percent or more of the Asian Indian work force consists of recent immigrants. Naturally, they remain unfamiliar with the American economic system, the "market" so to say. They are "alien" faces to the prospective American employer. The Asian Indian names sound unfamiliar to him. His/her non-White, non-Black "appearance" is not quite familiar. The accent he uses in speaking English is quite different. The way he wears his hat if he does it at all, or the way she wraps her 'sari' create certain communication barriers. The problem of communication is worst when the Asian Indian immigrant offers to be hired without any schooling in the United States. Both the buyer and the seller begin the negotiation with limited knowledge of each other, and the net result is a "fractured" market.[3] Note that they both are speaking the English language, and still they fail to communicate with each other. It is far more than the traditional language gap. Indeed, a host of non-market factors contribute to the tilt of the economic profile of Asian Indians. The magnitude of the tilt remains to be determined.

The second contributing factor works in a rather complicated way. The Asian Indian, even after the liberalization of the Immigration and Naturalization Laws in the 1960's, can immigrate here with "priority" based on professional standing and technical skill. Many of them came here when there was a relative shortage of physicians; then engineers when the labor market here needed more of them; at other times, the new immigrants were scientists. Needs vary, and job descriptions of the prospective immigrants vary. The superior technical skill of the new immigrant often becomes the friction point. For reasons stated earlier, the Asian Indian immigrant often begins by accepting an economic status which he/she soon discovers to be a state of underemployment. True, successive generations of immigrants began accepting what may be termed less than competitive economic profiles, and then went on to work hard to move up in their careers. This familiar format of career advancement for an immigrant works well with those who immigrate here with little technical skill. Higher professional and technical backgrounds which enabled many Asian Indians to become immigrants in the first place soon become a critical tension point. The tension, as it is allowed to be built up, makes the individual less productive. The individual is soon perceived

as lacking team spirit. It hurts the individual's career advancement. It thus contributes to a further negative tilt to the enconomic profile of Asian Indian Americans.

Indeed, the two issues are intertwined. Even when the Asian Indian can successfully clear himself/herself of the initial "screening" by the potential employer, he/she still has a real problem in obtaining a few references. His former employer is far off in India, and in any case is not likely to be known here. He/she does not belong to a local church or temple. He/she has not been a member of a "club," and has little access to the political and social leadership here. He/she soon induces himself/herself to accept an offer far less than competitive lest any chance to "enter" into the American market vanish or become unduly delayed. The point is a moot one: the entry or the "access" to the market is not "free" to this immigrant. Thus, the economic profile which is based on a summary of many such individual profiles can very reasonably be poorer than what it would otherwise have been. True, there are exceptions, and we have no reason to minimize the glory of some success stories.

As the individual continues to move up for further career advancement, the process of peer evaluation becomes a continuous process, and naturally so. Again, the Asian Indian may fail to be the beneficiary of free and open peer evaluation. Social barriers, perceived and/or real, persist, and he/she is still an alien. This kind of problem is of course less acute for Asian Indians who had schooling here, and certainly for those who are born here. One's native-born spouse can be a help. Perhaps there is no exception. The peer evaluation process remains constrained. It is certainly nothing very special for Asian Indians. It has been found to be so for women, for the Blacks, and also for many other groups. The built-in on-job discrimination researchers have detected to be real for other non-prime labor groups. Many Asian Indian immigrants must continue to be haunted by the terrible memory that back in India as members of the prime labor group of the country, they might have knowingly or unknowingly given support to such on-job discriminatory practices to various other non-prime labor groups.

Here in the United States, the Asian Indian

immigrant lacks the common sharing of the Greco-Roman culture and the Judeo-Christian experience. Most of his peers who have the task of periodically evaluating his professional standing cannot but see him as quite different from them. It makes a difference, and thus the eventual economic profile that emerges for the group as a whole can be so affected. Chadda[1] and Ishikawa[7] in two independent studies have suggested that underemployment, not unemployment, appears to be a more serious problem for the Asian Indian and the Japanese American groups. Both suggest that career advancement constitutes a critical problem for the two Asian American groups.

Any scientific effort to develop an economic profile of Asian Indian Americans can be successful only if we first disestablish some of the myths that continue to haunt many.[5] The myth of all such myths, in my view, is the widely held belief that Asian Indians have had no history of disadvantage. They are perceived to have had their journey to this land of affluence the easy way. This is far from true. The real truth is the 1917 Asian Exclusion Act, and the closing of the gates of America to all immigrants from Afghanistan to Korea, the "forbidden" Asia. The disadvantages of nonentry and/or "restricted quota" of immigration are real, and any attempt to deny history is certainly no way to search for truth.

If restricted immigration quotas over the years until the late 1960's are seen as conservative road-blocks, the liberals have their own share of myths too. They are the architects of the much-quoted phrase "brain drain." The Asian Indian immigrant is seen as a "brain drain" by the so-called liberal school, and his/her emigration from India is seen to be a grave loss to India's progress and prosperity. If the experiences of European nations which have historically witnessed successive waves of emigration of their peoples to the United States provide any evidence, truth must be seen to lie in the fact that both continents on the two shores of the Atlantic have made enormous economic gains by this process of emigration. The world as a whole would have been a much poorer place to live in if successive rounds of emigration from Europe to America had never taken place. The Asian Indian need not, and must not share any sense of

guilt, and thus press for the best bargain he/she can get.

In today's fast moving interdependent world, both labor and capital are global factors of production. They are internationally mobile, and such factor mobility, unrestricted and globally competitive, can contribute to the greater prosperity of the world as a whole. The choice between "brain drain" and its total extinction by prolonged non-use is quite obvious. The proper perspective is to study economics of export of human capital and the return flow of goods and services. The "brain drain" is at best an idle slogan to re-establish the Ricardian theory of free mobility of goods, but not of factors of production in international trade. Today, capital mightily flows across the frontiers of nations, and international flow of human capital also has become an important fact.

One more popular myth we must deal with here. The myth is that Asian Indians have success assured. There exists a recent quick study somewhere in the United States Government which lends credence to this myth. Unfortunately, this myth also finds support from two other sources.

First, the quick facile studies by some social scientists, based on limited data base often describe the Asian Indian economic profile in glowing terms. A study based on listings in "Who is Who Among Indian Immigrants" can hardly be a scientific profile, since the data base begins by excluding everybody who is not "anybody." Others have indulged in comparing say the median family income of Asian Indians living in the New York Metropolitan area with the U.S. national median family income. No adjustments for age, education, professional background have been provided. One would like to read about "controlled" comparisons of economic profiles of comparable groups. Since a very large number of Asian Indian immigrants are physicians, a controlled study of the economic profile of this group vis-à-vis the same of a group of immigrant physicians from Europe will be of interest. Even then, adjustments must be made for years of immigration and such other factors, which will correct for income differentials relative to areas of specialization amongst the physicians. Both these "controlled" groups then can be compared with a group of native White physicians.

The second group of researchers who contribute to this myth consists of many and varied individuals who often work with no well-defined design of research. For example, it is an absurd research design, to say the least, when one compares the earnings profile of Asian Indian immigrants with that of their peers who have remained back in India, or with what they would have earned if they were still working in India. The same absurd findings will be obtained if one compares the earnings profile of an immigrant group from any other European country with that of a related group who have remained in the original country. It makes little sense to compare family income median of Irish Americans with that of people in Ireland, or to compare the economic profile of Italian Americans with that of people in Italy. The scientific basis of any such study must relate the economic profile of a non-prime labor group, in the present case of Asian Indian Americans, with that of the prime labor group in the American market, i.e. the White male in prime age group.

Based on a cross section random sample of 300 Asian Indians, Chaddha[1] reported a perception of job discrimination amongst Asian Indian immigrants. A similar study by Elkhanialy and Nicholas[6] about Asian Indian immigrants reported that an overwhelming majority of their respondents, who were Asian Indian professionals, felt that job discrimination exists and hurts them.

It is important to note here that the 1970 U.S. Census tabulations showed that the median family income of the three Asian American groups — the Chinese, the Filipino and the Japanese, compared favorably with the U.S. national family income median. Indeed, these three groups were seen to be doing "better" than the national average. Yuan-li Wu[13] writes: "The large number of poor Chinese, especially in Chinatowns, have somehow escaped the full attention of those concerned with the plight of minorities. These Chinese Americans have managed to survive through a high participation rate in the labor force. According to the 1970 census, 59 percent of Chinese American families had two or more income earners, which compared with 51 percent for White families." Betty Lee Sung[12] concludes: "The substantially lower personal income figures (for Chinese Americans) reveal a more accurate measure," and she therefore rejects the finding that the Chinese family median income is higher than the U.S. national family median income as a "deceptive" measure. Roberto S. Mariano[8] argues: "At first glance, aggregate data from the 1970 census may indicate that Asian Americans are well off in terms of income, employment, education, and return to schooling. However, appropriate adjustments should be introduced for the presence of multiple workers in Asian American families, as well as for geographic regions since most Asian Americans are located in high cost-of-living areas in the United States." Sen[11] and Sato[10] present independent evidence to show that adjustments for school years will reveal a relatively lower earnings profile for the Asian Indians and the Japanese American groups.

A preliminary scrutiny of Asian Indian data shows that in most families both spouses work, therefore any measure of median family income without adjustment for the number of family members working will be a "deceptive" measure. Further careful adjustments for years of schooling, age, and professional specialization, must be incorporated before an unbiased economic profile can be constructed. For Asian Indians in the United States, participation of women in the work force is very high. In a large majority of Asian Indian families, both spouses are professional. Kanta Marwah[9] extends the investigation to Asian Indian women by way of developing her hypothesis of tri-minority — women, foreign born, first generation immigrant, and finally a foreign born, first generation immigrant from an Asian country. Literature on sexual discrimination on the job is well known and extensive. Its extended application to Asian Indian women is called for before any attempt to construct an economic profile for the Asian Indians can be meaningfully undertaken.

The extent and intensity of the state of under-employment of Asian Indian Americans remain uninvestigated. The 1980 census data will provide an opportunity to undertake such an exercise. Methods of appropriate adjustments for education, age, sex, years of schooling, professional specialization, years of immigration, native born vis-à-vis foreign born, and areas of residence have been discussed by different researchers in different contexts. One must carefully draw upon them so that a substantive research design developed.

"Controlled" comparisons of Asian Indian immigrants' economic profile with that of immigrants from European countries, corrected for years of immigration, can be instructive, in terms of shedding some light on the impact of socio-cultural factors on relative earnings profiles. Immigrants from European countries share the same socio-cultural background as of the majority population of the country, who constitute the prime labor force. Needless to add that the definition of "prime" labor force, as referred to here, is the one that has been adopted by the U.S. Department of Labor. One can then extend the "controlled" comparisons further, and compare the two economic profiles, so developed, one of Asian Indian immigrants and another of immigrants from European countries, with that of the native White Americans. A straightforward comparison of Asian Indian economic profile with that of the U.S. national profile will be "deceptive," because data on earnings profiles of other disadvantaged groups, Blacks, Hispanics, American Indians, introduce a substantial downward bias in the global all-national measure of economic profile.

IV. CITIZENSHIP STATUS AND ECONOMIC PROFILE

It is a crisis of some magnitude when it comes to making the decision about citizenship status. The Asian Indian immigrant often prefers the continued status of a resident alien in the United States. Legally, he/she elects to remain a citizen of the Republic of India. An individual must exercise his/her fundamental right in this regard. The question had been debated if the resident alien, non-citizen status (living off the Green Card as commonly stated) could make any difference in an individual's economic profile. No simple answer to this difficult question is available. We can only make some conjectures.

Among other criteria, commitment and continued availability must be taken into consideration when an individual is up for review for his/her upward career advancement. There is no way of saying if a 'citizen' employee is more committed than an 'alien' one. However, it is possible to conclude that a citizen is preferred to an alien, if, of course, other things are equal. Again, there is generally an argument that an alien employee may at any time return to his/her homeland, and as such he/she earns a lower ranking when it comes to the criterion of continued availability. It is rather difficult to argue convincingly that a citizen employee may often be more unavailable for a given employer. Even though we cannot offer any conclusive argument, we suggest that the issue is of importance, and must be investigated.

It is generally believed that a resident alien Indian immigrant, who is an Indian citizen, might not have received equal employment opportunity considerations from his employer anytime the political relationship between India and the United States came under strain. Even in a state of normal peaceful friendly relations between the two countries, the same individual is subject to certain disabilities from which his counterpart from a military alliance country is exempt under the law of the land. The individual might have found it out late. These are no reasons to affect one's decision as to how one exercises one's right to citizenship. But, one must remain aware of certain basic facts.

If one has a complaint of job discrimination as an Asian Indian resident alien one is fully entitled to the protection of such affirmative action programs as may exist under law. But each individual has to seek redress in the court of law, and the law of the land is supposed to work by way of unfolding its majestic command in due course. But then, the individual must at some point ask himself/herself a question: is he/she asking for the best of both worlds? As a citizen of the Republic of India, the individual has assured himself/herself the privileges of the majority back in India. As a resident alien in the United States, he/she is exercising the right to protection as a minority group of immigrants. There is absolutely nothing unlawful in this dualism of experiences for the individual. The issue is not one of legal import, and the individual must find an answer for himself/herself to this real question.

The political protection is different from the protection the court of law grants to an individual. As a non-citizen resident alien, the Asian Indian has very limited access to the country's political leadership. As a non-citizen, the individual has voluntarily chosen to remain outside the political system of the country of his/her residence. He/she is not a part of the mainstream of the American political system. Thus the one and only appeal the Asian Indian non-citizen, resident alien has to the country's political system is based on humanitarian grounds. It often works, thanks to the American system. It cannot be made to work as a matter of one's right.

The simple point here is that the economic profile of Asian Indian immigrants in their adopted homeland is likely to be substantially intertwined with their citizenship status. Any research to construct an economic profile of the group must take this important facet into consideration. It has often been suggested that when the chips are down, Asian Indians, even if they are citizens of the United States, will be hurt. Were not thousands of Japanese Americans put in concentration camps during World War II? But then how many of us seriously believe that we will witness yet another Pearl Harbor? Let our maintained hypothesis be that we have made progress, and that never again will we let history repeat itself in all its barbaric atrocities.

V. Conclusion

In conclusion, it must be emphasized that the importance of a study of the economic profile of the Asian Indian segment of the American labor force must be seen in economic terms. There is more to it than race, sex, religion, and source of immigration. The basic issue is the gainful employment and full utilization of each component of a nation's labor force and manpower. Labor is not a simple, homogeneous factor of production. Extensive research has recently been done in the area of labor and manpower economics, and economics of human capital, in terms of its many heterogeneous components.

The American economy must optimize its economic gain, and economically rationalize its policy of immigration. America's manpower policy has historically been related to its immigration policy, and it has been related in sound economic terms. The "pie" of our gross national product (GNP) must be made to be the maximum, thus justifying our policy of letting in certain numbers of immigrants to join our labor force every year. A failure to adopt a sound economic policy will be responsible for our having to share a smaller "pie" with a larger number of people, a relative state of poverty. In addition, it may add to our social costs in the future. Of course, there are exceptional humanitarian grounds when our immigration policy must be allowed to deviate from other market considerations.

For the present case, it will be sound economic policy to ensure that we gainfully employ 200,000 adult employable immigrants of Asian Indian heritage. If and only if they are enabled to be most productive, the American economy will have gained most. The issue is basically one of scientific manpower management and must be viewed as such.

BIBLIOGRAPHY

*   Manoranjan Dutta is Professor of Economics at Rutgers — The State University of New Jersey, New Brunswick, NJ 08903.

1. Chaddha, Roshan L., "Problems and Perspectives of Career Advancement — A Cross-Section Survey of Asian Indians" (mimeo) This study was initially sponsored by the Association of (Asian) Indians in America in 1977. Stanford Workshop, August 20-25, 1978.

2. Dutta, M., Evidence Before the U.S. House of Representatives Subcommittee on Census and Population, June 1-2, 1976, No. 94-80, pp. 33-37.

3. _____, "Fractured Employment Market for the Asian/Pacific Americans" (mimeo) Stanford Workshop, 1978. An earlier version of the paper was presented at the National Conference on Asians in America and Asian Americans, City University of New York, New York, May 13, 1978.

4. _____, Evidence Before the U.S. Senate Subcommittee on Census and Population, March 1, 1979.

5. _____, "Asian/Pacific American Employment Profile: Myth and Reality — Issues and Answers" in *Civil Rights Issues of Asian and Pacific Americans: Myths and Realities,* May 8-9, 1979, U.S. Commission on Civil Rights, Government Printing, Washington, DC, 1980, pp. 445-494.

6. Elkhanialy, Hekmat and Ralph Nicholas, *Racial and Ethnic Self-Identification and Desire for Legal Minority Status Among Indian Immigrants in U.S.A.* University of Chicago Press, Chicago, Illinois, 1977.

7. Ishikawa, Mamorou, "Discrimination in Employment of Asian Americans" (mimeo) Stanford Workshop, 1978.

8. Mariano, Roberto S., "Problems and Perspectives: Towards a National Survey of the Socio-economic and Demographic Characteristics of Asian Americans" (mimeo) Stanford Workshop, 1978.

9. Marwah, Kanta, "Employment Status and Earnings Profile of the Tri-Minority Professionals — Non-native, Asian, Female" (mimeo) Stanford Workshop, 1978.

10. Sato, Kazuo, "The Asian American Employment Market: The Pattern and Prospects: The Japanese Experience (mimeo) Stanford Workshop, 1978.

11. Sen, Tapas K., "The Profile of U.S. Employment Market: Race, Ethnicity, Sex Mix" (mimeo) Stanford Workshop, 1978.

12. Sung, Betty Lee, *Chinese American Manpower and Employment,* Department of Asian Studies, City College of New York, New York, 1975.

13. Wu, Yuan-Li, *The Economic Condition of Chinese Americans* (forthcoming).

Some Statistics on Asian Indian Immigration
to the United States of America

by

S. Chandrasekhar

An evaluation of the migration phenomenon — be it demographic, economic, social or political — from the sending and/or receiving country, is possible if some reliable statistics of at least four categories are available. Ideally these are (a) a continuing individual register; (b) recording migrations when and as they occur; (c) querying people about their place of birth, previous residence and/or past migration; and (d) data by the residual method.

Unfortunately, the only official data generally available on international migration are the records of arrivals and departures of citizens, aliens and various other categories of a particular country which are maintained at sea and air ports of entry or government posts on land frontiers, passport and visa records, manifests of ships entering or leaving a country, and other related documents.

In 1783 the United States signed a peace treaty with England and began life as an independent, sovereign nation. And from that year on, all aliens entering the country with the intention of settling permanently were classified as immigrants, irrespective of their national origin. That is, the English, Scotch and Irish who came as colonial subjects or colonial immigrants now became immigrants like anyone else.

The United States federal government began to collect immigration statistics in 1820, following the passage of the Immigration Act of March 2, 1819, which required that masters of ships arriving at American ports declare the number, age, sex, occupation, former residence, destination, and nationality of their passengers. Unfortunately, however, these manifests were not always complete, consistent or correct. The quality of the data did not improve until the end of the First World War.

Today, statistics of United States immigration and emigration are collected and published by the Immigration and Naturalization Service, which belongs to the Department of Justice or what is called in most countries the Ministry of Law and Justice. Here is another difficulty — the Immigration and Naturalization Service is not a data collecting department like the Census Bureau, but a law-enforcing agency, and as such does not apparently devote much time or attention to the qualitative aspect of its work dealing with immigration data. A student of American immigration statistics must, however, sympathize with the Agency's difficulties and limitations.

While the statistics of arrivals and departures from the U.S. sea and air ports are fairly reliable, those collected at the land frontiers in the south and north leave much to be desired. The checks at the Canadian frontier are more a formality than anything, on the assumption that Canadians are not rushing into the U.S. as illegal immigrants.

On the other hand, however, a 1,550 mile-long land frontier between the United States and Mexico has not proved an effective barrier against the illegal immigration of Mexican citizens into the United States. The problem is of such serious proportions that, incredible as it may sound, numbers of illegal Mexicans in the U.S. are estimated to be anywhere between five and ten millions. Apparently the Immigration and Naturalization Service has neither the funds nor the personnel to patrol the difficult frontier.

Then there are some cases — it is difficult to estimate the magnitude — of aliens working on foreign vessels who "jump ship" and disappear within the country.

Despite these limitations, the official statistics of alien arrivals as immigrants or otherwise give some idea of the magnitude of immigration from any one country at any particular point of time. The emerging picture may be looked at more as a trend than as a curve of absolute numbers. And the figures are not always comparable over a long period of time, for the arrivals reflect the changes in immigration legislation.

TABLE 1
IMMIGRANT ARRIVALS IN THE UNITED STATES OF PERSONS REPORTING INDIA
AS A NATION OF LAST PERMANENT RESIDENCE:
1820-1977[1]

Year	Number	Year	Number	Year	Number	Year	Number
1820	1	1860	5	1900	9	1940	3
1821	—	1861	6	1901	20[2]	1941	—
1822	1	1862	5	1902	84	1942	—
1823	—	1863	1	1903	83	1943	1
1824	1	1864	6	1904	258	1944	—
1825	—	1865	5	1905	145	1945	196
1826	1	1866	17	1906	271	1946	550
1827	1	1867	2	1907	1,072	1947	318
1828	3	1868	0	1908	1,710	1948	198
1829	1	1869	3	1909	337	1949	177
1830	—	1870	24	1910	1,782	1950	107
1831	1	1871	14	1911	517	1951	104
1832	4	1872	12	1912	165	1952	130
1833	3	1873	15	1913	188	1953	128
1834	6	1874	17	1914	172	1954	159
1835	8	1875	19	1915	82	1955	187
1836	4	1876	25	1916	80	1956	202
1837	11	1877	17	1917	69	1957	214
1838	1	1878	8	1918	61	1958	379
1839	—	1879	15	1919	68	1959	302
1840	1	1880	21	1920	160	1960	243
1841	1	1881	33	1921	353	1961	352
1842	2	1882	10	1922	223	1962	476
1843	2	1883	9	1923	156	1963	975
1844	1	1884	12	1924	154	1964	425
1845	—	1885	34	1925	45	1965	549
1846	4	1886	17	1926	50	1966	4,670
1847	8	1887	32	1927	51	1967	3,764
1848	6	1888	20	1928	38	1968	4,057
1849	8	1889	59	1929	56	1969	7,412
1850	4	1890	43	1930	51	1970	9,823
1851	2	1891	42	1931	65	1971	16,483[2]
1852	4	1892[3]	—	1932	50	1972	13,085
1853	5	1893	0	1933	1	1973	11,197
1854	—	1894	0	1934	—	1974	12,890
1855	6	1895	0	1935	—	1975	15,198
1856	13	1896	0	1936	—	1976	16,549
1857	1	1897	0	1937	9	1977	18,613
1858	5	1898	0	1938	1		
1859	2	1899	17	1939	2		

1. U.S. Bureau of the Census. *Historical Statistics of the United States, Colonial Times to 1970* (Washington, D.C., 1975) pp. 107-108.

2. Long-term Emigrants and Immigrants by Country or Area of Last or Intended Long-Term Residence, 1958-1976. United Nations, *UN Demographic Yearbook,* 1977 (New York, 1978) pp. 612-626.

3. Included in "all other countries" — not published separately.

TABLE 2
IMMIGRANT ARRIVALS TO THE UNITED STATES, BORN IN INDIA
FOR EACH DECENNIAL CENSUS, 1870-1970[1]

Census Year	Number
1970	51,000
1960	12,296
1950	NA
1940	NA
1930	5,850
1920	4,901
1910	4,664
1900	2,031
1890	2,143
1880	1,707
1870	586

1. U.S. Bureau of the Census, *Historical Statistics of the United States, Colonial Times to 1970* (Washington, D.C., 1975) pp. 117-118.

TABLE 3
IMMIGRATION TO THE UNITED STATES FROM INDIA,
FOR DECADES 1820-1978[a]

Decade/Year	Number of Immigrants	Decade/Year	Number of Immigrants
1820	1	1951-1960	1,973
1821-1830	8	1961-1970	27,189
1831-1840	39		
1841-1850	36	1971-1975	66,650
1851-1860	43	1976	16,130
1861-1870	69	TQ 1976[b]	4,128
1871-1880	163	1977	16,849
1881-1890	269	1978	19,145
1891-1900	68		
1901-1910	4,713		
1911-1920	2,082		
1921-1930	1,886	Total,	
1931-1940	496	159 years,	163,698
1941-1950	1,761	1820-1978	

SOURCE: U.S. Department of Justice, Immigration and Naturalization Service, *Statistical Yearbook of the Immigration and Naturalization Service, 1978* (Washington, D.C.: U.S. Government Printing Office, 1979).

a. From 1820-1867, figures represent alien passengers arrived; from 1868-1891 and 1895-1897, immigrant aliens arrived; from 1892-1894 and 1898 to the present time, immigrant aliens admitted. Data for years prior to 1906 relate to country whence alien came; thereafter, to country of last permanent residence.

b. For 1971-76, data are for fiscal year ending June 30; 1977 and 1978 figures are for fiscal year ending September 30; and TQ 1976 is the transistion quarter July-September 1976.

TABLE 4
PERSONS OF INDIAN BIRTH
ADMITTED TO THE UNITED STATES, 1971-1978

Year	Total	Immigrants[a]	Non-immigrants[b]
1971-1975	354,823	72,912	281,911
1976	94,777	17,487	77,290
TQ 1976	33,486	4,569	28,917
1977	98,099	18,613	79,486
1978	121,363	20,753	100,610

SOURCE: See Table 3.

    a.   The definition here differs from that for Table 3; the Table 3 definition covers immigrants whose last permanent residence was India, whereas Table 4 figures are for persons born in India. The latter figure is slightly higher.

    b.   Students and others entering with multiple entry documents are counted only on first admission. This category of nonimmigrants includes temporary visitors (see Table 9).

TABLE 5
IMMIGRANTS FROM INDIA ADMITTED
TO THE UNITED STATES, 1978, BY CLASSES[a]

Class	Number	Percentage
Total immigrants admitted	19,145	100
Total immigrants subject to numerical limitations	17,467	91
Eastern hemisphere	17,454	91
Western hemisphere	13	0
Total immigrants exempt from numerical limitations	1,678	9
Parents of U.S. citizens	632	3
Spouses of U.S. citizens	640	3
Children of U.S. citizens or of spouses of U.S. citizens	191	1
Other classes	215	2

SOURCE: See Table 3.

    a.   Definition of immigrants from India same as in Table 3.

TABLE 6
IMMIGRANTS FROM INDIA ADMITTED TO THE UNITED STATES
UNDER NUMERICAL LIMITATIONS, BY PREFERENCE, 1978[a]

Preference	Number	Percentage
Total immigrants under limitations	18,967	100
Total relative preferences	14,171	75
1st preference: unmarried sons and daughters of U.S. citizens and their children	12	0
2nd preference: spouses, unmarried sons and daughters of resident aliens and their children	5,149	27
4th preference: married sons and daughters of U.S. citizens and their spouses and children	81	0
5th preference: brothers and sisters of U.S. citizens and their spouses and children	8,929	47
Total occupational preferences	3,777	20
3rd preference: professionals,	1,147	6
their spouses and children	1,454	8
6th preference: other workers,	763	4
their spouses and children	413	2
7th preference	2	0
Nonpreference immigrants	1,017	5

SOURCE: See Table 3.

a. Immigrants with India as the state of chargeability.

TABLE 7
IMMIGRANTS OF INDIAN BIRTH ADMITTED TO THE UNITED STATES IN 1978,
BY MAJOR OCCUPATION GROUPS[a]

Occupation Groups	Number of Immigrants
Total, all occupation groups	20,753
Professional, technical and kindred workers	4,731
Managers and administrators, except farm	1,121
Sales Workers	220
Clerical and kindred workers	742
Craftsmen and kindred workers	329
Operatives, except transport	326
Transport operatives	27
Laborers, except farm	51
Farmers and farm managers	24
Farm laborers and farm foremen	389
Service workers, except private household	187
Private household workers	42
Housewives, children, and others with no occupation reported	12,564

SOURCE: See Table 3.

a. Definition of immigrants from India same as in Table 4.

TABLE 8
IMMIGRANTS OF INDIAN BIRTH ADMITTED TO THE UNITED STATES IN 1978, BY SEX AND AGE

Age Group	Total	Male	Female
Total, all ages	20,753	11,185	9,568
Under 5 years	1,560	779	781
5- 9 years	1,411	719	692
10-19 years	2,049	1,016	1,033
20-29 years	8,363	4,187	4,176
30-39 years	4,657	3,024	1,633
40-49 years	1,565	935	630
50-59 years	597	271	326
60-69 years	413	177	236
70-79 years	118	66	52
80 years and over	20	11	9

SOURCE: See Table 3.

TABLE 9
NON-IMMIGRANTS OF INDIAN BIRTH ADMITTED TO THE UNITED STATES IN 1978, BY CLASSES

Class	Number of Non-immigrants
Total, all classes	100,610
Foreign government officials	606
Temporary visitors for business	9,344
Temporary visitors for pleasure	42,681
Transient aliens	8,173
Treaty traders and investors	169
Students	3,202
Spouses and children of students	331
International representatives	1,622
Temporary workers and trainees	356
Spouses and children of temporary workers and trainees	129
Representatives of foreign information media	38
Exchange visitors	,009
Spouses and children of exchange visitors	468
Fiancees of U.S. citizens	40
Children of fiancees of U.S. citizens	5
Intracompany transfers	211
Spouses and children of intracompany transfers	133
NATO officials	3
Returning resident aliens	32,090

SOURCE: See Table 3.

TABLE 10
ALIENS OF INDIAN BIRTH
WHO REPORTED UNDER THE ALIEN ADDRESS PROGRAM, 1976-1979

Status	1976	1977	1978	1979
Total	97,702	108,596	113,246	125,630
Permanent residents	83,191	95,557	98,148	113,879
Other than permanent residents	14,511	13,039	15,098	11,751

SOURCE: U.S. Department of Justice, Immigration and Naturalization Service, *Annual Reports,* 1976, 1977, 1978, 1979 (Washington, D.C.: U.S. Government Printing Office).

TABLE 11
THE ASIAN INDIANS IN THE UNITED STATES OF AMERICA (1980)

According to the preliminary results of the 1980 U.S. Census there were 361,544 Asian Indian Americans in the U.S. They constituted about two-tenths of one percent of the total American population of 226.5 million.

The regional dispersion of Asian Indians is as follows:	
North East	120,761 (33%)
North Central	85,119 (24%)
South	83,586 (23%)
West	72,078 (20)%

Asian Indians are concentrated in the following five states:	
New York	60,511
California	57,989
Illinois	35,711
New Jersey	29,507
Texas	22,226

ADDITIONAL MISCELLANEOUS INFORMATION
ABOUT INDIAN IMMIGRATION TO THE UNITED STATES

1. Immigrants in 1978 went primarily to urban areas in New York (3,173), California (3,100), Illinois (2,897), New Jersey (2,479), Pennsylvania (1,071), and Texas (1,034).

2. Aliens reporting under the alien address program in 1978 also were concentrated in these six states: New York (19,402), Illinois (11,968), California (11,108), New Jersey (10,968), Pennsylvania (5,397), and Texas (5,258).

3. In 1978, 6,476 Indians were naturalized, 3,959 males and 2,517 females. In addition 240 administrative certificates of citizenship were issued to realtives of newly naturalized citizens.

4. In 1978, 4,475 aliens of Indian birth were adjusted to permanent resident status.

5. From 1946 to 1978, 140 Indians have been admitted as refugees.

6. In 1978, 46 Indians were deported and 365 were required to depart, due to improper entry or failure to comply with regulations for aliens (e.g., failure to renew papers, failure to report).

A Bibliography of Asian Indians in the United States: History of Immigration and Immigrant Communities in the United States

Compiled by

S. Chandrasekhar

Abstracts of the Reports of the Immigration Commission, 64th Congress, 3rd Session, Senate Document 747, Vol. 1 (Washington, 1911).

Ahmad, Bashir, "Indian Students in the Melting Pot of an American Campus," M.S. Thesis, University of Wisconsin, 1971.

Allchin, Bridget and Raymond. *The Birth of Indian Civilization* (Harmondsworth: Penguin, 1968).

Allen, Katheryn Martin, "Hindoos in the Valley," *Westways*. 31:3 March 1945.

———, "Hindoos in the Valley," *Westways* XXXVII April 1937.

Ames, Michael M. and Joy Inglis, "Conflict and Change in British Columbia Sikh Family Life," *British Columbia Studies* (BC Studies). No. 20, Winter 1973-74.

(The) Annals. American Academy of Political and Social Science. *The New Immigration.* Sp. Edn., Edward P. Hutchinson, 1966.

"Anti-Oriental Riots," *The Independent*. 63:3067, September 12, 1907.

Arasaratnam, S. *Indians in Malaysia and Singapore* (London: Oxford University Press, 1970).

(The) Asian Experience in North America. An Arno Press Collection (New York: Arno Press, 1978).

(The) Asiatic Exclusion League Proceedings (January, March, April, September, October 1910; January, March 1911).

Auerbach, Frank J. (Revised Third Edition By Elizabeth J. Harper and Ronald F. Chase), *Immigration Laws of the United States* (New York: Bobbs-Merrill, 1975).

Avery, Edwina A., and C.R. Gibson. *Laws Applicable to Immigration and Nationality* (Washington, D.C., 1953).

Awasthi, S.P., "Manpower Aspects of American Immigration Laws" *Manpower Journal*. Oct.-Dec. 1967.

Baden, Anne L. *Immigration into the U.S.: A Select List of Recent References* (Washington, D.C. 1953).

Bagai, Leona B. *The East Indians and the Pakistanis in America* (Minneapolis: Lerner Publications, 1967).

Bahr, Chadwick Strauss. *American Ethnicity* (Boston: D.C. Heath, 1979).

Banerjee, Kalyan Kumar. *Indian Freedom Movement: Revolutionaries in the United States of America* (Calcutta: 1969).

———. *Indian Freedom Movement: Revolutionaries in America* (Calcutta: Jijnasa, 1969).

———, "East Indian Immigration into America," *Modern Review* (November 1964).

Barrier, N.G., "Punjab Politics and the Disturbances of 1907." Ph.D. dissertation, Duke University, 1966.

Barth, Gunther. *Bitter Strength: A History of the Chinese in the United States, 1850-1870* (Cambridge, Mass.: Harvard University Press, 1964).

Beetham, D. *Transport and Turbans* (London: Oxford University Press, 1971).

Bennet, Marion T. *American Immigration Policies, A History* (Washington: Public Affairs Press, 1963).

Bernard, William S., et al. (eds.). *American Immigration Policy: A Reappraisal* (New York: Harper, 1950).

Berry, Browton. *Race and Ethnic Relations*. 2nd Edition. (Boston: Houghton Mifflin, 1958).

Bhagat, G. *Americans in India: Commercial and Consular Relations, 1784-1860*. 2nd Edition (New York: New York University Press, 1971.)

Bharati, Aghenanda, "Sab/azād/sab/barbād," *The Illustrated Weekly of India* (Bombay) November 11, 1979.

Bilder, Z. Helen, "The East in the United States," *Great Britain and the East,* XLVIII (1937).

Bohning, W.R. *Basic Aspects of Migration from Rich to Poor Countries: Facts, Problems and Policies*. (Geneva: International Labor Organization, 1976).

Bose, Arun Coomer. *Indian Revolutionaries Abroad, 1905-1922: In the Background of International Developments* (Patna: Bharati Bhawan 1971).

Bose, Sudhindra, "Asian Immigration in the United States," *Modern Review* (Calcutta) XXV (May 1919).

_____, "American Impression of a Hindu Student," *Forum* LIII. 1915.

Bouscaren, Anthony T. *International Migration Since 1945* (New York: Praeger, 1963).

Bovenkerk, Frank. *The Sociology of Return Migration: A Bibliographic Essay* (The Hague: Martinus Nifhoff, 1974).

Bowles, Chester, "Indians in America and Americans in India," *Eastern Economist* (New Delhi) September 1, 1967.

Bradfield, Helen H., "The East Indians in Yuba City: A Study in Acculturation." M.A. thesis, California State University, Sacramento, California, 1971.

Bromwell, William J. *History of Immigration to the United States Exhibiting the Number, Sex, Age, Occupation and Country of Birth of Passengers from 1819 to 1855 Compiled from Official Data* (New York: Redfield, 1856.)

Brown, Francis J. and Joseph S. Roucek (eds.). *One America: The History, Contributions, and Present Problems of our Racial and National Minorities*. Rev. ed. (New York: Prentice Hall, 1952).

Brown, Emily C. *Har Dayal: Hindu Revolutionary and Rationalist* (Tucson: The University of Arizona Press, 1975).

Brown, Giles T., "The Hindu Conspiracy, 1914-1917," *Pacific Historical Review,* XVII:3 (August 1948).

Brunner, Edmund de S. *Immigrant Farmers and Their Children* (New York: Doubleday, 1929).

Bryce-Laporte, Roy S. *The New Immigrants: Their Origin, Visibility and Challenge to the American Public — Impact of the Immigation Act of 1965* (Washington, D.C. 1976).

Buchanan, Agnes Foster, "The West and the Hindu Invasion," *Overland Monthly,* LI (1908).

Burke, Marie Louise. *Swami Vivekananda in America, New Discoveries* (Calcutta: Advaita Ashrama, 1958).

California and the Oriental: Japanese, Chinese and Hindu. State Board of Control of California, Sacramento, 1922 (Report of Governor William D. Stephens of California to the Secretary of State).

California Statistical Abstract, (Sacramento: State Printing Office, 1975).

Canada. British Columbia. Legislative Assembly. *Report on Oriental Activities within the Province*. (Victoria, British Columbia: 1927).

Canada. Department of Labor. *Report of W.L. Mackenzie King on Mission to England to Confer with the British Authorities on the Subject of Immigration to Canada from the Orient and Immigration from India in Particular*. (Ottawa, Canada, 1908).

"Captain Stephen Phillips, 1764-1838," *Essex Institute Historical Collections,* Vol. 76 April (Salem, Mass: 1940).

Chadney, James G., "The Vancouver Sikhs: An Ethnic Community in Canada." Ph.D. dissertation. Michigan State University, 1976.

Chakravorti, Robindra C., "The Sikhs of El Centro: A Study in Social Integration." Ph.D. dissertation. University of Minnesota, 1968.

Chandras, Kananur V. (ed.). *Racial Discrimination Against Neither-White Nor-Black American Minorities* (San Francisco: R and E Research Associates, 1978).

Chandrasekhar, S., "The Movement of Asian People: A Challenge to the Churches" in *In A Strange Land*. Report of a World Conference on Problems of International Migration and the Responsibility of the Churches held at Leysin, Switzerland, June 11-16, 1961 (Geneva: World Council of Churches, 1961).

_____, *Hungry People and Empty Lands:* Population Problems and International Tensions (London: George Allen and Unwin, 1955) Third edition.

_____, "Indians in South Africa, II," *United Asia* (Bombay) April 1953.

_____, "Indians in South Africa, I," *United Asia* (Bombay) February 1953.

_____, "Indian Emigration to Borneo," *The Hindu* (Madras) March 2, 1951.

_____, "South African Indians: A Brief Survey," *The Modern Review* (Calcutta) August 1949.

_____, "Indian Immigration in America" in Clarence A. Peters (Compiled by) *The Immigration Problem* (New York: H.W. Wilson Co., 1948).

_____. *Indian Emigration to America* (Bombay: Oxford University Press, 1945) Pamphlet.

_____, "The Emigration and Status of Indians in the British Empire," *Social Forces* December 1945.

_____, "The Indian Community in the United States," *The Far Eastern Survey* (New York) June 6, 1945.

_____, "Indian Immigration in America," *The Far Eastern Survey* (New York) July 26, 1944.

_____, "The Population Problem in India," Ph.D. dissertation, New York University, 1944, Chapter VI (Ann Arbor: University of Michigan Microfilms).

_____, "Indian Emigration to the U.S.A.," *Indian Review* (Madras) December 1943.

_____, "Indian Emigration to the Americas," *Indian Review* (Madras) November 1943.

_____, "Indian Migration," *Crisis* (New York) June 1943.

Chase, Raymond and S.G. Pandit. *An Examination of the Opinion of The Supreme Court of The United States Deciding Against the Eligibility of Hindus for Citizenship.* (Los Angeles: Penker, Stone and Baird Co., 1926, privately printed and distributed).

Coelho, George V. *Changing Images of America: A Study of Indian Students' Perceptions* (Glencoe, Illinois: Free Press, 1958).

Copeland, Senator Royal S., "Hindus are White: A Plea for Fairplay to Americans" (New York: Hindu Citizenship Committee, 1926).

Corbett, D.C. *Canada's Immigration Policy — A Critique* (Toronto: University of Toronto Press, 1947).

Dadabhay, Yusuf, "Circuitous Assimilation Among Rural Hindustanis in California," *Social Forces,* XXXIII December, 1954.

Daniels, Roger, "American Historians and East Asian Immigrants," *Pacific Historical Review,* XLIII:4 November, 1974.

_____ and Harry H.L. Kitano. *American Racism: Exploration into the Nature of Prejudice* (Englewood Cliffs, N.J.: Prentice-Hall, 1970).

Das, Mary, "True Status of Hindus Regarding American Citizenship," *Modern Review,* (Calcutta) XLI 1927.

Datta, R.K., "Characteristics and Attitudes of Immigrant Indian Scientists and Engineers in the U.S.A.," *Journal of Scientific and Industrial Research* 34 No. 2 February, 1975.

Das, Rajani K. *Hindustani Workers on the Pacific Coast* (Berlin: Walter de Gruyter Co., 1923).

Das, Taraknath, "People of India and U.S. Citizenship," *India Today,* (New York) August, 1961.

————, "Stateless Persons in the U.S.A.," *Calcutta Review,* XVI July 1925.

————, "What is at the Back of the Anti-Asianism of the Anglo-Saxon World?" *Modern Review,* (Calcutta) XXXV 1924.

————, "American Naturalization Laws Against the Chinese, Japanese and Hindustanies," *Modern Review,* (Calcutta) XXXIV 1923.

Davids, Leo, "The East Indian Family Overseas," *Social and Economic Studies,* Vol. 13, No. 3 September 1964.

Davie, Maurice R. *World Immigration with Special Reference to the United States* (New York: Macmillan, 1949).

Davis, Merle, "The Orientals" in H.P. Fairchild (ed.) *Immigrant Backgrounds* (New York: John Wiley, 1927).

Dayal, R., "The Disabilities of Indians Abroad," *Modern Review,* (Calcutta) XLI 1927.

Dees, J.L. *Tagore and America* (Calcutta: The United States Information Service, 1961).

Deol, G.S. *The Role of the Ghadar Party in the National Movement* (Delhi: Sterling Publishers, 1969).

Desai, P.N. and D. Mehta, "Indians in America — Changing Patterns of Life," *India Times,* (Chicago) March 20, 1979.

————, "Indians in America — The Friendship Connection," *India Times,* (Chicago) May 1979.

Dev, Dharam Yash. *Our Countrymen Abroad* (Allahabad: All India Congress Committee, 1940).

Dhami, Sadhu Singh. *The Sikhs and Their Religion* (Vancouver: Khalsa Diwan Society, 1943).

Dignan, Don K., "The Hindu Conspiracy in Anglo-American Relations During World War I," *Pacific Historical Review,* XL 1971.

Dikshit, G.S., "Sudhindra Bose in America," *Journal of Karnataka University* (Social Sciences), 4-1968.

Divine, Robert A. *American Immigration Policy, 1924-1952.* (New Haven: Yale University Press, 1957).

Dodd, Werther, "Hindu in the Northwest," *World Today,* 13:1 July 1907.

Drury, Clifford M., "Hinduism in the United States," *Missionary Review,* New Series XXXIV 1921.

Dutta, M., "Myths and Realities: Asian American Employment Status" in *Myths and Realities: Civil Rights Issues Regarding Asian Pacific Americans* (Washington, D.C.: Civil Rights Commission, 1980).

East Indians in Foreign Countries — Bibliography (Washington D.C.: U.S. Library of Congress, 1921).

Eckerson, Helen F., "Immigration and Emigration, 1948," *Monthly Review,* VI (October). Immigration and Naturalization Service, Department of Justice. (Washington, D.C.: United States Government Printing Office, 1948).

Elkhanialy, Hekmat and Ralph W. Nicholas (eds.). *Immigrants from the Indian Sub-Continent in the U.S.A.: Problems and Prospects* (Chicago: India League of America, 1976) mimeographed.

Fairchild, H.P. *The Mistake of the Melting Pot* (Boston: Little Brown, 1926).

_____. *Immigration: A World Movement and Its American Significance* (New York: Macmillan, 1925).

Ferguson, Ted. *A White Man's Country: An Exercise in Canadian Prejudice* (Toronto: Doubleday Canada, 1975).

Field, Henry. *"M" Project for FDR: Studies on Migration and Settlement* (Ann Arbor, Michigan: Microfilms, 1962).

Fieldbrave, Theodore., "East Indians in the United States," *Missionary Review,* LVII June 1934.

Fisher, Maxine P. *The Indians of New York City* (New Delhi: Heritage Publishers, 1980).

Fluret, Anne K., "Incorporation into Networks Among Sikhs in Los Angeles," *Urban Anthropology,* 3:1 Spring 1974.

Forbes, Angus, "East Indians in Canada," *International Journal* (1947).

Francis, R.A., "B.C.'s Turbaned Tide," *Canadian Business,* 25, February 1952.

Friedman, E. and M. Selden (eds.). *America's Asia* (New York: Vintage, 1971).

Ganguly, A.B. *Ghadar Revolution in America* (New Delhi: Metropolitan, 1980).

Gandhi, Rajnikant S. *Locals and Cosmopolitans of Little India: A Sociological Study of the Indian Student Community at Minnesota, U.S.A.* (Bombay: Popular Prakashan, 1974).

Gardner, Ray., "When Vancouver Turned Back the Sikhs," *Vancouver Sun,* November 8, 1958.

Garis, Roy L. *Immigration Restriction: A Study of the Opposition to and Regulation of Immigration to the United States* (New York, 1927).

Garner, J.W., "Denationalization of American Citizens," *American Journal of International Law,* XXI 1927.

Ghadr: Report of the Senate Fact-Finding Committee of Un-American Activities to the 1953 Regular California Legislature (Sacramento: California State Printing Office, 1953).

Ghose, Sailendra Nath, "Deportation of Hindu Politicals," *Dial,* LXVII August 23, 1919.

Gompers, Samuel. *Meat vs. Rice: American Manhood Against Asiatic Cooliesm* (San Francisco: Asiatic Exclusion League, 1908).

Gordon, Milton M. *Assimilation in American Life: The Role of Race, Religion and National Origins* (New York: Oxford University Press, 1964).

Grant, Rev. K.J., "Among the Hindus of British Columbia," *Missionary Messenger* (1915).

Gupta, S.P., "The Acculturation of Asian Indians in Central Pennsylvania," Ph.D. dissertation, Pennsylvania State University, 1969.

_____, "Changes in the Food Habits of Asian Indians in the United States," *Sociology and Social Research,* October 1975.

Handlin, Oscar. *The Uprooted* (Boston: Little Brown, 1973).

_____. *A Pictorial History of Immigration* (U.S.) (New York: Crown Publishers, 1972).

_____. *The American People in the Twentieth Century* (Boston: Beacon Press, 1963).

_____. *Immigration as a Factor in American History* (New York: Prentice Hall, 1959).

Haskett, Richard C., "Problems and Prospects in the History of American Immigration," in *A Report on World Population Migrations as Related to the United States of America* (Washington, D.C., 1956).

Hay, Stephen N., "Rabindranath Tagore in America," *American Quarterly,* XIV 1962.

Hess, Gary R., "The Forgotten Asian Americans: The East Indian Community in the United States," *Pacific Historical Review,* XLIII 1974.

_____. *America Encounters India, 1941-1947* (Baltimore: Johns Hopkins Press, 1971).

_____, "The 'Hindu' in America: Immigration and Naturalization Policies and India, 1917-1946," *Pacific Historical Review,* XXXVIII February 1969.

"Hindu Invasion," *Colliers,* XLV March 26, 1910.

"(The) Hindu: The Newest Immigration Problem," *Survey,* XXV October 1, 1910

Hindus in California (Sacramento: The California State Board of Control, 1920).

Hinduism Comes to America (Chicago: Vedanta Society, 1933).

Historical Statistics of the U.S., Colonial Times to 1970. Part I. Bicentennial Edition, U.S. Bureau of the Census. (Washington, D.C.: U.S. Government Printing Office, 1975).

Holland, Sir Robert, "Indian Immigration into Canada: The Question of Franchise," *Asiatic Review* April 1943.

Hopkins, C.T. *Commonsense Applied to the Immigration Question* (San Francisco: Turnbull and Smith, 1869).

Hoyt, Edwin Palmer. *Asians in the West* (Nashville: T. Nelson, 1974).

Hugh, J. Johnson. *The Voyage of the Komagata Maru: The Sikh Challenge to Canada's Colour Bar* (Delhi: Oxford University Press, 1979).

Hundley, Norris (ed.). *The Asian American* (Santa Barbara, California: 1976).

Hutchinson, Edward P. *Immigrants and Their Children, 1850-1950.* Census Monograph Series (New York, 1956).

_____, "Immigration Policy Since World War I" in Benjamin Mun Ziegler (ed.) *Immigration, An American Dilemma* (Boston, 1953).

_____. *Current Problems of Immigration Policy* (Washington: American Enterprise Assn., 1949).

Immigration and Nationality Act, with Amendments and notes of Amendments and Related Laws, Committee Print, for the use of the House Judiciary Committee, Second Edition, revised September 1, 1960 (Washington, D.C., 1960).

Immigration and Nationality Act, Public Law 414, 82 Congress, Second Session (66 Stat. 163) (Washington, 1952).

Immigration Quota Areas According to Immigration and Nationality Act of United States: Map (Washington, D.C., 1961).

Immigration: Report of the Commission General for Immigration, 1919-1920 (Washington, D.C.: U.S. Government Printing Office, 1921).

Immigration War Brides Act (U.S. Code, December 28, 1945).

India Today, monthly bulletin published by the India League of America (J.J. Singh, President) New York City 1938-1947.

Ingersoll, Anna Josephine, "The Swamis in America," *Arena,* 22 October 1899.

Institute of Applied Manpower Research, New Delhi. *Migration of Indian Engineers, Scientists and Physicians to the United States.* Report 1966 (New Delhi, 1968).

Ireland, R.L., "Indian Immigration in the United States, 1901-1964," *Indian Journal of Economics* (Bombay), Vol. 46, April 1966.

Isemonger, F.C. and J. Slattery. *An Account of the Ghadr Conspiracy* (Lahore, Punjab: Supdt. of Printing, 1921).

Jackson, Carl Thomas, "The Swami in America," Ph.D. dissertation: University of California, Los Angeles, 1964.

Jacoby, Harold S., "More Thind Against than Sinning," *Pacific Historian,* 2:4 November 1958.

_____. *A Half-Century Appraisal of the East Indians in the United States* (Stockton, California: University of the Pacific, 1956).

Jain, Sushil Kumar, "East Indians in Canada," *Research Group for European Migration Problems Bulletin* (The Hague, P.H. Klop, June 1971).

_____. *East Indians in Canada* (Windsor, Ontario: 1970).

Jain, Usha R., "The Gujaratis in San Francisco," M.A. thesis, University of California, Berkeley, 1964.

Jayawardena, Chandra, "Migration and Social Change: A Survey of Indian Communities Overseas," *Geographical Review,* 58 July 1968.

Jensen, Joan M., "East Indians" in Stephan Thernstrom (ed.) *Harvard Encyclopedia of American Ethnic Groups* (Cambridge: Harvard University Press, 1980).

_____, "Federal Policy in the Shaping of Indian Occupations in the United States, 1900-1917." Unpublished paper delivered at the Western Conference of Asian Studies, November 1974.

_____, "Apartheid: Pacific Coast Style," *Pacific Historical Review,* 38:3 August 1969.

_____, "Outcasts in a Savage Land: The East Indians in North America," unpublished ms.

Jha, J.C. *Calcutta to Caroni: The East Indians of Trinidad.* John La Guerre (ed.) (Bristol, U.K.: Western Printing Services Ltd., 1974).

Johns, Watson L., "The Hindu in California," University of Oregon Seminar Paper, 1941.

Johnson, Annette Thackwell, "The Rag Heads — A Picture of America's East Indians," *The Independent.* 109, October 28, 1922.

_____, "Armageddon?," *The Independent.* 109, November 25, 1922.

Jones, Chester L., "Legislative History of Exclusion Legislation," *The Annals* (Philadelphia) September 1909.

Jones, Idwal, "Mr. Har Chand," *Westways.* 31:9, September 1939.

Jones, Maldwyn A. *American Immigration* (Chicago: 1960).

Josh, Sohan Singh. *Hindustan Gadar Party: A Short History.* 2 Vols. (New Delhi: People's Publishing House, 1977-1978).

_____. *Tragedy of Komagata Maru* (New Delhi: People's Publishing House, 1975).

_____. *Baba Sohan Singh Bhakna: Life of the Founder of the Ghadar Party* (New Delhi: People's Publishing House, 1970).

Juergensmeyer, Mark, "The International Heritage of the Ghadar Party," *Sikh Sansar,* 2:1, March 1932.

_____, "The Ghadar Syndrome: Nationalism in an Immigrant Community," *Punjab Journal of Politics,* 1:1, October 1977.

Juergensmeyer, Mark and N. Gerald Barrier (eds) *Sikh Studies: Comparative Perspectives on a Changing Tradition* (Berkeley: Graduate Theological Union, 1979).

_____, "The International Heritage of the Ghadar Party: A Survey of the Sources," in N.G. Barrier and Harbans Singh (eds.) *Punjab: Past and Present: Essays in Honor of Dr. Ganda Singh* (Patiala: Panjabi University Press, 1976).

Kamath, M.V. *The United States and India: 1776-1976* (Washington, D.C., The Embassy of India, 1976).

Kennedy, John F. *A Nation of Immigrants* (Revised) (New York: Harper and Row, 1964).

Khush, Harwant Kaur, "The Social Participation and Attitudes of the Children of East Indian Immigrants," M.A. thesis, Sacramento State College, 1965.

King, W.L. MacKenzie. *Report of the Royal Commission Appointed to Inquire into the Methods by which Oriental Laborers have been Induced to Come to Canada* (Ottawa: Government Printing Bureau, 1908).

_____. *Report on Mission to England to Confer with British Authorities on the Subject of Immigration to Canada from the Orient and Immigration from India in Particular* (Ottawa: Government Printing Bureau, 1908).

Klass, Morton. *East Indians in Trinidad: A Study of Cultural Persistence* (New York: Columbia University Press, 1961).

Komagata Maru. *Commission of Inquiry Report, 1914* (Calcutta: Government Printing Press, 1914).

Kondapi, C. *Indians Overseas, 1838-1949* (Bombay: Oxford University Press, 1951).

Konvitz, Milton R. *The Alien and the Asiatic in American Law* (Ithaca, New York: Cornell University Press, 1946).

La Brack, Bruce, "The Sikhs of Northern California," Ph.D. dissertation, Syracuse University, 1980.

_____, "Sikhs — Real and Ideal," in Juergensmeyer, Mark and Gerald Barrier (eds.), *Sikh Studies.* Berkeley Religious Studies Series, Graduate Theological Union (Berkeley: Lancaster-Miller Publishers, 1979).

_____. *Health Care and the East Indian.* Western Interstate Commission on Higher Education (available through Yuba-Sutter Health Department, Yuba City, California), 1975.

Lambert, Richard D. and Marvin Bressler, "Indian Students and the United States: Cross-Cultural Images," *The Annals,* (Philadelphia) September 1959.

_____. *Indian Students on an American Campus* (Minneapolis: University of Minnesota Press, 1956).

"Literatus" [Amal Home] "Rabindranath Tagore in America," *Modern Review,* XXI, Nos. 4, 5, 6, April, May, June 1917.

Littleton, C. Scott, "Some Aspects of Social Stratification Among the Immigrant Punjab Communities of California," *Culture Change and Stability* (Department of Anthropology, University of California, Los Angeles, 1964).

Lockley, Fred, "The Hindu Invasion," *The Pacific Monthly,* May 1907.

Loftis, Anne. *California — Where the Twain Did Meet* (New York: Macmillan, 1973).

Lovett, Robert Moses, "The United States and India: A Footnote to Recent History," *New Republic,* LXVI April 1, 1931.

Lowenthal, David and Lambrose Comitas, "Emigration and Depopulation, *Population Review,* (Madras) 6:2, 1962.

Lyman, Stanford M. *The Asian in the West* (Reno and Las Vegas: Desert Research Institute, University of Nevada, 1970).

M Project (1942-1945), ed. by Henry Field. *Studies on Migration and Settlement* (Washington, D.C.: Library of Congress, 1946).

MacArthur, Walter, "Opposition to Oriental Immigration," *The Annals,* September 1909.

Mackett, Walter C., "Some Aspects of the Development of American Opinion in India, 1918-1947," Ph.D. dissertation, University of Southern California, 1957.

Madhu, S.R., "Indians in America," *Span,* (New Delhi) September 1974.

Malcolm, Roy, "Immigration Problems on the Pacific Coast," *Current History,* XXXIII October 1930-March 1931.

Malik, Yogendra. *East Indians in Trinidad: A Study of Minority Politics* (London: Oxford University Press, 1971).

Maslog, Crispin Chio. *Filipino and Indian Students' Images of Themselves, of Each Other, and of the United States* (Minneapolis, 1967).

Mathur, L.P. *Indian Revolutionary Movement in the United States of America* (Delhi: S. Chand & Company, 1970).

Mayer, Adrian C. *A Report on the East Indian Community in Vancouver* (Vancouver: Institute of Social and Economic Research, University of British Columbia, 1959).

Mazumdar, Haridas Thakurdas. *America's Contribution to Indian Freedom* (Allahabad: Central Book Depot, 1962).

McKenzie, R.D. *Oriental Exclusion: The Effect of American Immigration Laws, Regulations and Judicial Decisions upon the Chinese and Japanese on the American Pacific Coast* (University of Chicago Press, 1928).

McWilliams, Carey. *Brothers under the Skin.* (Boston: Little Brown, 1951).

Meadows, Paul et al. *Recent Immigration to the United States: The Literature of the Social Sciences* (Washington, D.C.: Smithsonian Institute Press, 1976).

Mears, Eliot G. *Resident Orientals on the American Pacific Coast: Their Legal and Economic Status* (University of Chicago Press, 1928).

Melendy, Howard Brett. *Asians in America* (Boston: Twayne Publishers, 1977).

Memoranda regarding Hindus in the United States, January 23, 1914. U.S. Department of Commerce and Labor, Bureau of Immigration and Naturalization. File No. 52903/11B.

Millard, Bailey, "Rabindranath Tagore Discovers America," *The Bookman,* (New York) XLIV November 1916.

Miller, Allan P., "An Ethnographic Report on the Sikh (East) Indians of Sacramento Valley," unpublished ms. South/Southeast Asia Library, University of California, Berkeley.

Mills, H.A., "East Indians Immigration to British Columbia and the Pacific Coast States," *American Economic Review,* 1:1 March 1911.

_____, "East Indian Immigration on the Pacific Coast," *The Survey,* 28:9 June 1912.

Misrow, Jogesh C. *East Indian Immigration on the Pacific Coast* (San Francisco: R and E Research Associates, 1971) (originally published at Stanford, California, 1915).

Modern Review, (Calcutta) June 1914 (editorial).

Mohapatra, Mahindra Kumar, "Overseas Indians in Urban America: A Study of Their Attitudes and Experiences Involving Discrimination in American Society," *Nagarlok,* January-March 1979.

Moore, Adrienne. *Rammohun Roy and America* (Calcutta: Satis Chandra Chakravarti, 1942).

Morse, Eric W., "Some Aspects of the Komagatamaru Affair, 1914," *Canadian Historical Association Journal,* 1936.

_____, "Immigration Status of East Indians in Canada," Ph.D. dissertation, Queens University, Kingston, Canada, 1936.

Mukerji, Girindra, "Hindu in America," *Overland Monthly,* n.s. 51:4 April 1908.

_____, "The Hindu in America," *American Review of Reviews,* XXXVII May 1908.

Mukherjee, Radhakamal, *Migrant Asia* (Failli: Typografia, 1936).

_____. *Races, Lands and Food: A Program for World Subsistence* (New York: Dryden Press, 1946).

Mukherjee, Sujit. *Passage to America: The Reception of Rabindranath Tagore in the United States,"* Ph.D. dissertation, University of Pennsylvania, 1963.

Naidis, M., "Propaganda of the Gadar Party," *Pacific Historical Review,* Vol. 20 1951.

Nand, Prem, "Indians in Canada," (Calcutta) pamphlet n.d. 1915?

Nandi, Proshanta. *Quality of Life of Asian Americans* (Chicago: Pacific/Asian American Mental Health Research Center, 1980).

_____, "The Quality of Life of Asian Americans in Middlesize Cities: A Neglected Area of Research," *Bridge,* Vol. 5, No. 4.

Narayanan, R., "Indian Immigration and India League of America," *Indian Journal of American Studies,* (New Delhi) Vol. 2, No. 1, May 1972.

Nasser, Bush M., "Differential Adjustment between Two Indian Immigrant Communities in Toronto," Ph.D. dissertation, University of Colorado, 1974.

Natarajan, L. *American Shadow over India* (Bombay: People's Publishing House, 1952).

New Yorker, March 1951.

Olin, Spencer C., Jr., "European Immigrant and Oriental Alien: Acceptance and Rejection by the California Legislature of 1913," *Pacific Historical Review,* Vol. XXXV August 1966.

Pacific Coast Khalsa Diwan Society, *Annual Reports 1973-1974* (Stockton, California, 1973-1974).

Pandia, D.P. and Mme. Kamaladevi, "Justice for Hindus in America," *Christian Century,* LVII March 3, 1940.

Panikkar, K.M. *India, Past and Present* (Englewood Cliffs, N.J.: Prentice Hall, 1964).

Patel, Narsi, "A Passage from India," *Transaction,* 9:6 1972.

Paul, Gurbachan S., "The Stay or Return Decision of Indian Students," (a special case of international migration) Ph.D. dissertation, University of Oregon, 1972.

Pendleton, Edwin Charles, "History of Labor in Arizona Irrigated Agriculture," Ph.D. dissertation, University of California, 1950.

Petersen, William (ed.). *The Background to Ethnic Conflict* (Leiden: E.J. Brill, 1979).

Phillips, James Duncan. *Salem and the Indies* (Boston: Houghton Mifflin, 1947).

Plender, R. *International Immigration Law* (Leiden: Sijthoff, 1972).

Preston, William, Jr. *Aliens and Dissenters, Federal Suppression of Radicals, 1903-1933* (Cambridge: 1963).

Puri, Harish K., "The Ghadar Party: A Study in Militant Nationalism," Ph.D. dissertation, Guru Nanak Dev University, Amritsar, India, 1975.

Rajkumar, N.V. *Indians Outside India* (New Delhi: All India Congress Committee, 1950).

Ram, Chandra. *India Against Britain* (San Francisco: Hindustan Ghadr, 1916).

_____. *Exclusion of Hindus from America Due to British Influence* (San Francisco: Hindustan Ghadr, 1916).

Randhir, Singh. *The Ghadr Heroes* (Bombay: People's Publishing House, 1945).

Rathore, Naeen Gul, "Indian Nationalist Agitation in the United States: A Study of Lala Lajpat Rai and the Indian Home Rule League of America, 1914-1920," Ph.D. dissertation, Columbia University, 1965.

Reid, Robie L., "The Inside Story of the 'Komagatamaru'," *British Columbia Historical Quarterly,* Vol. 5 1941.

Report Annual. Commissioner General of Immigration since 1892 (Washington, D.C., Government Printing Office).

(A) Report on World Population Migrations as Related to the United States of America (Washington, D.C., George Washington University, 1956).

Reports. California Immigration Association. Pamphlets for various years before 1915.

Riggs, Fred W. *Pressure on Congress: A Study of the Repeal of Chinese Exclusion* (New York: King's Crown Press, 1950).

_____, "U.S. Legislation Affecting Asiatics," Part II, *Far Eastern Survey,* XVI May 21, 1947.

Ross, E.A., "The Causes of Race Superiority," *The Annals,* July 1901.

Saha, P. *Emigration of Indian Labor: 1834-1900* (Delhi: People's Publishing House, 1970).

Sajnani, Daulat N. (ed.). *Discover India in New York: An Indian Guide to Every Place in Town* (New York: Sajnani, 1977).

Salera, Virgil. *U.S. Immigration Policy and World Population Problems* (Washington, D.C.: American Enterprise Association, 1960).

Saran, P. and Edwin Eames (eds.). *The New Ethnics* (New York: Praeger, 1980).

Sareen, Tilak Raj. *Indian Revolutionary Movement Abroad, 1905-1921* (New Delhi: Sterling, 1979).

Saund, Dilip Singh. *Congressman from India* (New York: E.P. Dutton, 1960).

Saxton, Alexander. *The Indispensable Enemy: Labor and the Anti-Chinese Movement in California* (Berkeley: University of California Press, 1971).

Scheffauer, Herman, "The Tide of Turbans," *Forum,* XLIII June 1910.

Schisby, Marian, "Hindus and American Citizenship," *Proceedings of the National Conference on Social Work* (Chicago: University of Chicago Press, 1927).

Scott, Franklin D. (ed.). *World Migration in Modern Times* (Englewood Cliffs, N.J.: Prentice Hall, 1968).

Scott, James Brown, "Japanese and Hindus Naturalized in the United States," *American Journal of International Law,* XVII 1923.

Seth, Madan Gopal, "A Study of Attitudinal Change of Indian Students in the United States," Ph.D. dissertation, Boston University, 1960.

Shah, Khalid and Linda, "Indians in New York," *Illustrated Weekly of India* (Bombay), April 22, 1973.

Shankar, Richard Ashok, "Integration Goal Definition of the East Indian Students in the Sutter County Area," M.A. thesis, California State University, Chico, 1971.

Sihra, Nand Singh, "Indians in Canada," *Modern Review,* (Calcutta), XIII 1914.

_____, Balwant Singh and Narain Singh, "Indians in Canada: A Pitiable Account of Their Hardships by One Who Came from the Place and Knows Them," *Indian Review,* (Madras), XIV June 1913.

Silving, Helen. *Immigration Laws of the United States* (New York: Oceana Publications, 1948).

Singh, Anup, "Nationals of India in the U.S.A.," Washington, D.C., National Committee for India's Freedom, 1945.

_____, "A Quota for India Too," *Asia and the Americas,* XLIV April, 1944.

Singh, Diwakar Prasad, "American Official Attitudes Toward the Indian Nationalist Movement: 1905-1929," Ph.D. dissertation, University of Hawaii, 1964.

Singh, Gurdial, "East Indians in the United States," *Sociology and Social Research,* XXX 1946.

Singh, Gurdit. *The Voyage of the Komagatamaru* (Published by the compiler at 32 Asutosh Mukerjee Road, Calcutta. n.d.).

Singh, Harnam. *Indian National Movement and American Opinion* (New Delhi: Central Electric Press, 1962).

Singh, J.J., "Memorandum on Proposed Legislation to Authorize the Naturalization and Admission into the United States under a Quota of Eastern Hemisphere Indians of India," (New York: India League of America, 1945) (mimeographed pamphlet).

Singh, Khushwant. *A History of the Sikhs.* Vol. 1, 1469-1834; Vol. 2, 1839-1964 (Princeton: Princeton University Press, 1963, 1966).

Singh, Kushwant, and Satindra Singh. *Gadhar 1915: India's First Armed Revolution* (New Delhi: R and K Publishing House, 1966).

Singh, Pardaman. *Ethnological Epitome of the Hindustanees of the Pacific Coast* (Stockton: Khalsa Diwan Society, 1922).

Singh, Rattan. *A Brief History of the Hindustan Gadhar Party* (San Francisco, 1929).

Singh, Sant Nihal, "Asiatic Immigration: A World Question," *Living Age,* CCLXXXII 1914.

_____, "The Picturesque Immigrant from India's Coral Strand: Who He is and Why He Comes to America," *Out West,* XXX 1909.

_____, "Indians in America — Educated Indians in America," *Modern Review,* (Calcutta), III 1908.

Siu, Paul C., "The Sojourner," *American Journal of Sociology,* 58 July 1952.

Smillie, Emmaline E., "An Historical Survey of Indian Migration within the Empire," *Canadian Historical Review,* 4 1923.

Smith, Marian, "Sikh Settlers in Canada," *Asia and the Americas,* August 1944.

Smith, William C. *Survey of Race Relations on the Pacific Coast* (Salem: Oregon State Archives, 131 vols., 1924-1927).

Solanki, Ratilal, "Americanization of Immigrants: A Study in Acculturation of Asian Indians in the State of Colorado and the Educational Implications," Ph.D. dissertation, University of Denver, 1973.

Spellman, John W., "The International Extensions of Political Conspiracy as Illustrated by the Ghadr Party," *Journal of Indian History,* 31 1959.

Spengler, J.J., "Issues in American Immigration Policy," *The Annals,* American Academy of Political and Social Science, March 1958.

Spicer, E.H., "Acculturation," *International Encyclopedia of Social Sciences,* 1:21-27 1968.

State Board of Control of California. Report to Governor William D. Stephens, *California and the Oriental: Japanese, Chinese and Hindus* (Sacramento, 1920).

Stern, Bernard S., "American Views of India and Indians 1857-1900," Ph.D. dissertation, University of Pennsylvania, 1956.

Stidger, C.P. *Our Immigration Law: Its Menace to American Citizenship* (San Francisco: Allen Printing Co., 1913).

Strobel, Bill, "California Sikhs: The Pride and the Prejudice," *California Today,* The Magazine of the San Jose Mercury News, May 27, 1979.

Study of Population and Immigration Problems by Subcommittee No. 1 of House Judiciary Committee, *Asian Populations: The Critical Decades.* Presented by Irene B. Taeuber, Special Series No. 4, Washington, D.C., 1962.

Taft, Donald R. and Richard Robbins. *International Migrations: The Immigrant in the Modern World* (New York: Ronald Press, 1955).

Tagore, Rabindranath, "Race Conflict," *Modern Review,* XIII April 1913.

Tandon, Prakash, "An Indian Turns American: The Problems of a Generation Caught Between Two Cultures," *Times of India,* (Bombay), July 6, 1980.

Telleen, Judy G. Johnson. *A Predictive Model of the Cumulative Academic Achievements of Graduate Students from India* (Ann Arbor: University of Michigan School of Education, 1971).

Third World Population in California. Office of Lieutenant Governor, Council on Intergroup Relations, Intern Research Project (Sacramento, California, 1977).

Thomas, Wendell Marshall. *Hinduism Invades America* (New York: Beacon Press, 1930).

"United States vs. Bhagat Singh Thind, Decided February 19, 1923," *Supreme Court Reporter,* 43:10 April 1, 1923.

United States Code Annotated, Title 8, *Aliens and Nationality,* 8:1182:11. (St. Paul, Minnesota: West Publishing Co., 1977).

U.S. Congress, House. Committee on Immigration and Naturalization. *To Grant a Quota to Eastern Hemisphere Indians and to Make Them Racially Eligible for Naturalization.* Hearings before the Committee on Immigration and Naturalization, House of Representatives, 79th Congress, 1st. Session (March 7, 8, 13, 14). (Washington, D.C.: U.S. Government Printing Office, 1945).

U.S. Congress, House. Committee on Immigration and Naturalization. *Hearing, Restriction of Immigration of Hindu Laborers.* 63rd. Congress, 2nd. Session (February 13 to April 30). (Washington, D.C.: U.S. Government Printing Office, 1914).

U.S. Congress, Senate. Committee on Immigration. *To Permit all Persons from India Residing in the U.S. to be Naturalized.* Hearings before a subcommittee of the Committee on Immigration, (April 26), 79th Congress, 1st Session, (Washington, D.C.: U.S. Government Printing Office, 1945).

U.S. Department of Commerce. Bureau of the Census. 16th Census of the United States: 1940, Vol. II, Part I. *Characteristics of the Population: Summary.* (Washington, D.C.: United States Government Printing Office, 1943).

_____. 15th Census of the United States: 1930, Vol. II. *General Report, Statistics by Subjects.* (Washington, D.C.: United States Government Printing Office, 1933).

U.S. Department of Commerce and Labor, Commissioner-General of Immigration, *Annual Report, 1911-1913; 1915-1920.*

U.S. Department of Justice, Immigration and Naturalization Services, *Annual Report.* (Washington, D.C.: U.S. Government Printing Office, for various years).

U.S. Immigration Commission. *Report on Japanese and East Indians on the Pacific Coast,* 1910.

_____. *Hearings on the Hindu Immigration 1914.* Three Parts, 63rd. Congress, 2nd Session.

_____. Part 25 in three volumes. Senate Document 85. Japanese and East Indians. Part 1, 2, 3. U.S. Senate Document 208.

_____. *Report: Immigrants in Industries.* (Senate Document 633. Immigrants in Industries. Twenty-five parts. Part 25. Senate Document 85, ''Japanese and East Indians, Part 1, 2, 3), (Washington, D.C.: U.S. Government Printing Office, 1907).

_____. *Reports of the Immigration Commission: Review of Immigration, 1820-1910; Distribution of Immigrants, 1850-1900,* S. Doc. No. 756, Serial 5878, 61st. Congress, 3rd. Session. Washington, D.C., 1911.

United States Industrial Commission. *Reports of the Immigration Commission,* 41 vols., (Washington, D.C.: 1900).

United States Senate, 61st. Congress, 2nd. Session, Document 633, Reports of the Immigration Commission. *Immigrants in Industry,* pt. 25, *Japanese and Other Immigrant Races in the Pacific Coast and Rocky Mountain States,* Vol. 1, *Japanese and East Indians.* (Washington, D.C.: Government Printing Office, 1911).

Urbahns, T.D. *History of Agriculture in Sutter County.* Transcription of lecture by County Agriculture Commissioner on deposit with Sutter County Library (Yuba City, California, n.d.).

Voice of India, a monthly magazine edited by Dr. Anup Singh and published by the National Committee for India's Freedom (Washington, D.C., 1944-1947).

Waiz, S.A. *Indians Abroad.* Foreword by L. Nartarajan, 2nd. ed. (Bombay: Imperial Citizenship Association, 1927).

Waldron, Gladys H., ''Anti-Foreign Movements in California, 1919-1929,'' Ph.D. dissertation, University of California, Berkeley, 1945.

''War with Great Britain?'' *Outlook,* LXXXVII September 14, 1907.

Weller, Judith Ann. *The East Indians Indenture in Trinidad.* (Rio Piedras, Puerto Rico: Institute of Caribbean Studies, University of Puerto Rico, 1968).

Welty, Paul Thomas. *The Asians.* 3rd edn. (Philadelphia: Lippincott, 1970).

Wenzel, Lawrence A., ''The Rural Punjabis of California,'' *Phylon,* LX:29 February 1968.

_____, ''East Indians in Sutter County,'' *North State Review,* III 1968.

_____, ''The Identification and Analysis of Certain Value Orientations of Two Generations of East Indians in California,'' Ph.D. dissertation, University of the Pacific, 1966.

Wharton, Don, ''They Are Forging a New Link with India,'' *Reader's Digest,* LXXIV February 1959.

Wherry, E.M., ''Hindu Immigrants in America,'' *Missionary Review of the World,* XXX 1907.

Whitehill, Walter Muir. *The East Indian Marine Society and Peabody Museum of Salem* (Salem: Peabody Museum Papers, n.d.).

Whom We Shall Welcome. Report of the (U.S.) *President's Commission on Immigration and Naturalization* (Washington, D.C.: U.S. Government Printing Office, 1953).

Wood, Louise Ann, ''East Indians in California: A Study of Their Organizations, 1900-1947.'' M.A. thesis, University of Wisconsin, 1966.

Yuba City Gurdwara Committee *Annual Reports — 1971-1976.* (Yuba City, California, 1971-1976).

ABOUT THE CONTRIBUTORS

Brown, Emily C.

B.A. Ohio State Univ.; M.A. Arizona State Univ.; Ph.D. Univ. of Arizona; Asst. Prof., Far East Area Studies of the American Graduate School of International Management, Glendale, Arizona, 1950-60; Asst. to President, Univ. of Arizona, 1960-61; Fullbright Senior Lecturer, U.S. Educational Foundation, at Literacy Village, Lucknow, India, 1961-62; Associate Professor and Professor, Indian History, University of Northern Iowa, 1966-69. Her publications include *Har Dayal: Hindu Revolutionary and Rationalist* (Tuscon: Arizona Univ. Press, 1974). Has contributed papers on Non-Gandhian nationalism, Punjab politics, expatriate nationalists and India's immigrants in the U.S. She spent 1969-70 in India researching her book on Har Dayal.

Chandrasekhar, Sripati

B.A. (Hons.) Presidency College, Madras; M.A., Univ. of Madras; Ph.D., New York Univ. 1944. Professor and Chair, Economics Dept., Annamalai Univ. 1947-51; Director, Demographic Research, UNESCO, Paris, 1948-49. Professor and Chair, Economics Dept., Baroda Univ. 1951-55; Nuffield Foundation Fellow, London School of Economics, 1953-55; Director, Indian Institute of Population Studies, Madras, 1955-66; Visiting Lecturer, Univ. of Penna. 1944-45; Visiting Prof. of Demography, Univ. of Missouri, 1956-57; Visiting Prof. of Population, Univ. of Pittsburgh, 1961-62; Visiting Prof. of Sociology, Univ. of California, Riverside, 1964-65; elected Member of Upper House of Indian Parliament, 1964-70; Minister of Health and Family Planning, Govt. of India, 1966-70; Visiting Professor of Demography, Univ. of Delhi, 1967-68; Visiting Fellow, Battelle Research Center, Seattle, 1970-72; Distinguished Visiting Prof. of Sociology, San Diego State Univ. 1972-73, Visiting Prof., School of Public Health, UCLA, 1973-74; Regents Lecturer, Univ. of California, Santa Barbara, 1974; Vice-Chancellor and Pres., Annamalai Univ., 1974-80; Lucy Stern Trustee Prof. of Sociology, Mills College, Oakland, Calif., 1979; Visiting Professor, California State Univ., Hayward, 1980; currently teaches at Univ. of California, Irvine. Author of numerous books and papers on population and family planning. Has lectured before conferences and universities in some 130 countries. Has received several awards, honors, and doctorates *honoris causa.* Now divides his time between Madras and La Jolla, CA.

Dutta, Manoranjan

B.A. and M.A. Calcutta Univ.; Ph.D. Univ. of Penna., 1962; Professor of Economics, West Bengal Education Service till 1958; Fulbright-Smith-Mundt Fellow, 1958-59; Ford Foundation Fellow, 1959-60; taught at Univ. of Rhode Island and Univ. of Puerto Rico. Currently Prof. of Economics at Rutgers - The State Univ. of New Jersey. His books include *Econometric Methods* (Cincinnati: South Western Publishers, 1975), co-Editor, *Essays in Regional Economic Studies* (Durham, N.C.: Acorn Press, 1982); *The New Perspective of the U.S. - India Economic Cooperation* (forthcoming). Contributing author, *The Brookings Quarterly Econometric Model of the United States (1965); Civil Rights Issues of Asian/Pacific Americans: Myths and Realities* (1980). His articles have appeared in *International Econ. Review, Review of Econ. and Stat., Econometrica, Empirical Economics,* and *Economic Mathematique.* He has been a member of the 1980 Census Advisory Committee for Asian/Pacific American Population, 1976-80.

Hess, Gary R.

B.A. Univ. of Pittsburgh; M.S. and Ph.D. Univ. of Virginia. He did research in India under a Fulbright grant, and has been a member of the History faculty at Bowling Green State University since 1964; Chairman of the Department from 1973-1982 and was Acting Dean of the College of Arts and Sciences in 1981-82. His books include *America Encounters India,* (Johns Hopkins Press, 1971) and his articles have appeared in the *Journal of American History, Pacific Historical Review, Current History, Diplomatic History, Agricultural History,* and *Southern Studies.* He is currently completing a book on American involvement in Southeast Asia during the 1940s.

Jacoby, Harold S.

A.B., College of the Pacific; M.A. Northwestern Univ.; Ph.D. Univ. of Penna.; Prof. Sociology, Univ. (College) of the Pacific; Dean, College of the Pacific; Also taught at Yamaguchi Univ., Japan; Millsaps College, Mississippi. Author: *Half-Century Appraisal of East Indians in the United States* (1956) "Some Demographic and Social Aspects of Early East Indian Life in the U.S." in *Sikh Studies,* 1979. With War Relocation Authority, Tule Lake, Ca., and Chicago, 1942-44; United Nations Relief and Rehab. Admin., Egypt, Palestine, and Kenya, 1944-46. Retired 1976.

Juergensmeyer, Mark

B.A. Univ. of Illinois; M.A. Union Theological Seminary, N.Y.; Ph.D. Univ. of California, Berkeley; Project Director, Center for South Asian Studies, Berkeley; Visiting Professor, Punjab University, 1966 and 1970-71; currently Associate Professor of Religious Studies at the Graduate Theological Union and the University of California, Berkeley; among his books, M. Juergensmeyer and N.G. Barrier (eds.) *Sikh Studies: Working Papers of the 1976 Summer Conference* (Berkeley: Religious Studies of America, 1978) and author, *Religion as Social Vision: The Movement against Untouchability in 20th Century Punjab* (Berkeley: Univ. of Calif. Press, 1982). His articles have appeared in professional and popular periodicals.

La Brack, Bruce

B.A. and M.A., Univ. of Arizona; M. Phil and Ph.D. Syracuse Univ. 1980. Taught at the Univ. of Northern Iowa, 1970, and the Univ. of Nebraska, 1970-72. Language Fellow, American Institute of Indian Studies, New Delhi, 1969-70; National Science Foundation Grantee, 1974-75. Currently Associate Professor of Anthropology and International Studies, Univ. of the Pacific; Fulbright Research Award, Japan-U.S. Educational Commission for Tokyo-based International Education project. Has contributed several papers to professional and popular periodicals on California Sikhs and related subjects.

Leonard, Karen

B.A., M.A. and Ph.D. (1969) Univ. of Wisconsin; Univ. of Wisconsin scholar in India (1962); has taught at the Univ. of San Diego (1969-70); National Defense Foreign Language Fellow, India and England, 1962-66; Faculty Research Fellow, American Institute of Indian Studies, India (1970-71); Assistant Professor in Indian History, Univ. of Virginia (1978); Director of Women's Studies, UCI 1978-79. Currently Associate Professor, Social Relations, Univ. of California, Irvine. Author of *Social History of an Indian Caste: The Kayasths of Hyderabad* (University of California Press, Berkeley and Oxford University Press, New Delhi, 1978). Has contributed several papers to professional and popular periodicals. Her articles have appeared in *American Anthropologist, Journal of Asian Studies, Signs* and *Pacific Affairs.*

INDEX

A

Accuracy of Statistics, 86
Afghanistan, 27, 39
American Federation of Labor, 16, 41
Apte, S.S., 47
Arabia, 18
Asia Pacific Triangle, 24, 25
Asiatic Barred Zone, 18
Asiatic Exclusion League, 30, 36, 41
Asian Indians, 76, 77
    alien religious mores, 81
    brain drain, 81
    economic profile, 79
    employment, 80
    immigrants admitted by
        preference, 90
    immigrant arrivals, 87
    in the U.S. in 1980, 92
    median income, 81
    non-immigrants admitted, 91
    regional distribution, 78
    Select Bibliography, 93-106
    unfamiliar names, 80
Assimilation of immigrants, 26, 33
Azad, Prithvi Singh, 57

B

Bailey, Thomas A., 41, 46
Baldwin, Roger, 32
Ballantine, Harry, 13
Banerjee, K.K., 34, 40
Bangladesh, 27
Barakatullah, 49
Baroda, 13
Barrier, N.G., 55
Barth, P. Gunther, 27
Bellingham, 29
Bentley, Rev. William, 12, 27
Bhakna, G. S. Singh, 49, 57
Bhutan, 27
Bode, H.E., 13
Bose, A.C., 55
Boston lakes, 13
Boxer rebellion, 42
Brar, Pratap S., 74
British Columbia, 19, 29, 46
British imperialism, 18
Brown, Emily C., 41, 52
Buck, Pearl S., 32
Bureau of Customs, 38
Burlingame, Anson, 15
Burlingame Treaty, 15
Burma, 18

C

California Alien Land Law, 31, 51
Caminetti, A., 29, 36
Canada, 19, 25, 29, 59
Canton, 16
Celler, Emmanuel, 32
Chadda, R.L., 82
Chan, Sucheng, 75
Chandra, Ram, 29, 49, 53, 57
Chandrasekhar, S., 11, 26, 34, 86
Chenchiah, B., 57
Chico, Nan, 26
Chinese Americans, 16
Church, D.S., 29
Citizenship, 20
Cleveland, President Grover, 19
Colonialism, 49
Commission, Dillingham, 18

D

Dadabhay, Y., 65, 67, 74
Daniels, Roger B., 34, 40, 66
Darling, Malcolm, 55
Das, R.K., 34, 46, 50, 55, 74
Das, Taraknath, 34, 56
Data Collection, 86
Davie, M.R., 27, 39
Dayal, Har, 29, 43, 45, 46-48, 50-53
Denmark, 21
Deol, G.S., 55
Deportation of aliens, 41
Desai, V.G., 57
Dickstein, Samuel, 33
Dutta, M., 76, 84

E

East India Company, 12
East India Marine Society, 12
East Indians, see Asian Indians
Einstein, Albert, 32
Elkhanialy, H., 85
Ely, Edward, 13, 27
Everett, 29

F

Farnham, Benjamin, 14
Ferguson, Ted, 57
Fisher, Louis, 32
Flint, Senator Frank, 36
Free immigration, 11
Fresno, 70
Fulbright, Senator J.W., 33

G

Gandhi, M.K., 53, 57
Gentlemen's Agreement, 16, 39
Germany, 43-45
Gibaut, Capt. J., 12
Gokhale, S.L., 21
Gore-Hama, 17
Government of India, 25
Great Britain, 21
Greece, 21
Gujaratis, 13, 66
Gujarati Patels, 65

H

Handlin, Oscar, 17, 27
Hardas, Balshastri, 47
Hawaii, 17, 38
Heer, David, 26
Hess, Gary R., 29, 34
Higgs, Robert, 75
Higham, John, 27
Holland, 25, 67

I

Imperial Valley, 70
India, 18, 25
Indians, (Asian) in U.S.
    California Sikhs, 59
    citizenship status, 83
    economic profile, 76
    ethnic anger, 4
    ethnicity of wives, 71
    family life, 67
    Gadar as ethnic identity, 53
    Gadar newspapers, 43, 44, 55, 57
    Gadar party, 29, 30, 43, 44, 45, 48
    Gurudwara, 51
    Hindi association, 51
    Hindu association, 43
    Hindusthan association, 51
    Khalsa Diwan Society, 53
    Marriages, 67
    revolution for freedom, 41
    Sikhs, 19, 27, 43, 48, 51
    Sikh marriages, 68
    Sikh-Catholic marital mores, 72
    Sikh-Mexican marriages, 70
    Sikh-Muslim marital mores, 73
    Sikh vital statistics, 68
    statistics of immigration, 87-92
    Yuguntur ashram, 43, 51

Indonesia, 18
Italy, 21

J

Jacoby, H.S., 27, 35, 59, 74
Japanese Americans, 17-18, 82
Japanese Exclusion League, 36
Jensen, Joan M., 42, 46, 55, 65
Johnson, President L.B., 25, 66
Josh, Sohan Singh, 55
Juergensmeyer, M., 48, 55

K

Kennedy, President John, 24, 25
Kennedy, Senator Edward, 11, 26, 28
Kennedy, Senator Robert, 25
Keefe, Daniel J., 36
Kenya, 13
King, W.L. MacKenzie, 65
Kite, Elizabeth S., 34
Komagata Maru, 27, 44, 50, 57
Korean Exclusion League, 36
Kung, S.W., 27
Kwantung, 16

L

La Brack, Bruce, 52, 59
Lal, G.B., 52
Langer, Senator William, 32
Lazarus, Emma, 36
Leonard, Karen, 67, 74
Literacy test, 19, 39
Looseley, Allyn C., 75
Luce, Clare Booth, 23, 32

M

Malawi, 13
Malay States, 18
Mamoru, I., 85
Mariano, Robert S., 82
Marwah, Kanta, 82, 85
Marysville, 64
Master, S.M., 15
Mathur, K.P., 34, 55
Mazumdar, A.K., 31
McCarthy, Senator Joseph, 54
McWilliams, Carey, 66, 75
Mehta, F., 12
Melendy, H. Brett, 27
Merwanji, D., 13, 15
Mexican Americans, 32, 60, 73
Mexican War, 1846-48, 16
Miller, Stuart C., 27

Millis, H.A., 29, 34
Morse, Eric W., 47, 65
Murarka, R., 74

N

Naoroji, D., 12
Nehory, E.J., 15
Neibuhr, Reinhold, 32
Nepal, 27
New Jersey, 11
New York, 11
Nicholas, R., 85

O

O'Dwyer, M. Francis, 47
Ozawa case, 20, 29, 30, 31
Ozawa, Takao, 20

P

Pacific Barred Zone, 18
Pandit, S.G., 20, 21, 28, 31, 75
Parsis, 12-15
Pavalko, R.M., 27
Pennsylvania, 11
Perry, Commodore, M.C., 17
Petersen, William, 26
Philippines, 23, 38, 39
Poland, 21
Polynesian Islands, 18
Portugal, 25
Punjabi language, 74
Puri, Harish K., 55, 56

R

Ramspeck, R., 33
Rhodesia, 13
Roosevelt, President Theodore, 17, 35
Ruef, Abraham, 17
Russell, Richard B., 33
Russia, 21

S

Sacramento, 70
Sainsara, G.S., 55
Salem, Madras State, 11
Salem, Mass., 11
Sandmeyer, E.C., 27
Sarabha, K. Singh, 49, 52
Sargent, Frank P., 36
Sato, Kazuo, 85
Saund, D.S., 58
Scandinavia, 21

Scheffauer, H., 34
Schmitz, Eugene, 17
Seattle, 29
Sen, Tapas, K., 85
Shanghai, 67
Sharma, S.R., 55
Siam, 18
Sikkim, 27
Singh, Anup, 104, 106
_____ Bhagvan, 49, 53, 57
_____ Ganda, 55
_____ Harbans, 55
_____ J.J., 98
_____ J. Lab, 74
_____ Jwala, 49
_____ Khushwant, 46, 55
_____ Narrak, 55
_____ Saint Nihal, 34
_____ Satindra, 55
_____ Veer, 19
Sri Lanka, 27
Stockton, 70
Sun, Yat-sen, 54, 55
Sung, Betty Lee, 27, 85
Surat, 13
Sutherland, George, 20

T

Taft, President William Howard, 39
Taylor, Paul S., 75
Thind, Bagat Singh, 20, 31, 34
Thind case, 19, 27, 31
Tripathi, D., 15, 27
Truman, President Harry S., 24, 34, 65

U

United States
    First arrival from India, 12
    Parsis plan to immigrate, 12
    Alien Act of 1798, 27
    Alien Contract Labor Law, 16, 17
    Burlingame Treaty, 15
    Census questionnaire, 1980, 77
    Chinese exclusion, 35
    Chinese Exclusion Act, 14, 15, 35, 41
    Department of Labor, 83
    Free immigration, 15
    Immigration and Naturalization
        Service, 86
    Immigration Act of 1907, 17
    Immigration Act of 1917, 18
    Immigration Act of 1924, 15, 21
    Immigration Act of 1926, 23
    Immigration Act of 1940, 22
    Immigration Act of 1952, 23

Immigration Act of 1965, 11, 24, 25
Immigration statistics, 86
Internal Security Act of 1950, 24
Lees v. U.S., 17
State Immigration Law, 11
Supreme Court, 12
Thind case, 19, 27, 31
Undocumented aliens, 86
U.S. v. Ajhoy Kumar Mazumdar, 31
U.S. v. Balsara, 3, 20, 31
U.S. v. Bhagat Singh Thind, 27, 31
U.S. v. Franz Bopp et al, 46
U.S. v. Ozawa, 20
U.S. v. Sakharam Ganesh Pandit, 31

V

Vancouver, 44
Van Fleet, William C., 47
Van Groenou, W., 26

W

Washington, President George, 10
Washington State, 29
Webster, Daniel, 13, 27
Wenzell, Lawrence A., 34
West Indies, 25
Whitehall, W.M., 27
Wilson, President Woodrow, 29, 39, 45, 75
Wolverton, Charles E., 20
Wu, Yuan-li, 82, 85

Y

Yuba City, 64

Z

Zambia, 13

"A Dirty, Filthy Book"

The Writings of Charles Knowlton and Annie Besant on Birth Control and Reproductive Physiology and an Account of the Bradlaugh-Besant Trial

BY S. CHANDRASEKHAR

This history of the struggle to disseminate birth control information in England includes the Bradlaugh-Besant edition of Knowlton's *Fruits of Philosophy* and two of Besant's pamphlets on birth control.

* * * * *

This valuable reference work on the evolution of the birth control movement in England and her colonies in the 19th century is a lucid survey . . . This work provides a comprehensive overview and includes a useful bibliography. Even more valuable is his excellent discussion of the impact of the movement on India.

CHOICE

Professor Chandrasekhar has performed a valuable service to all students and advocates of free speech as well as planned parenthood by reproducing Knowlton's *Fruits of Philosophy* and putting the landmark Bradlaugh-Besant Trial that emerged from their publication of it into historic context. His *"Dirty Filthy Book"* is a masterfully clean job of creative research and scholarship.

Stanley Wolpert, Ph.D.
Professor of History
University of California, Los Angeles

In these days when our freedoms, which make America the great country it is, are being challenged by ignorant bigots, every American would do well to examine Chandrasekhar's important *"A Dirty Filthy Book"* which describes what it took to make progress in the recent past. Those committed to freedom of choice in birth control and family planning will be fascinated with its contents.

George C. Denniston, M.D.
President, Population Dynamics
Seattle, Washington

232 Pages, Illustrations, Notes, Bibliography, Index. $16.95

UNIVERSITY OF CALIFORNIA PRESS

Berkeley, Los Angeles, New York, London.